Ready to Run

Dr. Kelly Starrett
with T.J. Murphy

*Unlocking Your
Potential to
Run Naturally*

Victory Belt Publishing

Las Vegas

This book is for Juliet. Thank you for the effortless way you continually save my life. Here's to the death of the notion that evolution, innovation, and creativity happen as solo events. A lion is nothing without a cheetah.

First published in 2014 by Victory Belt Publishing Inc.

ISBN-13: 978-1-628600-09-4

The information included in this book is for educational purposes only. It is not intended or implied to be a substitute for professional medical advice. The reader should always consult his or her healthcare provider to determine the appropriateness of the information for his or her own situation or with any questions regarding a medical condition or treatment plan. Reading the information in this book does not create a physician-patient relationship.

Victory Belt® is a registered trademark of Victory Belt Publishing Inc.

Cover Design: Tom Wiscombe. TomWiscombe.com

Photo Credits
Caragh Camera: 15, 21, 30, 38, 57, 64, 88, 121, 122, 166, 265
Glen Cordoza: 63, 65
Serge Dubovsky: 39, 96, 99, 100, 108, 148, 179, 183, 186, 203, 255, 261
Darren Miller: 2, 6, 27, 41, 113, 271, 275-276. Darrenmillerphoto.com
John Segesta: 18-19, 31, 40, 50, 52, 54, 54, 55, 64, 66, 68-69, 80, 82, 86, 92-95, 105-107, 114-118, 124-142, 149-165, 172-178, 190-193, 200-202, 205-254, 260, 264, 270. Johnsegesta.com
Courtesy of Rock and Roll Marathon: 110
Courtesy of CrossFit, Inc: 48, 143, 167, 259. CrossFit.com
Courtesy of MobilityWOD: 15, 21, 30, 38, 39, 57, 88, 96, 99, 108, 121, 122, 148, 166, 179-189, 203, 255, 261, 265. MobilityWOD.com

Printed in the USA
RRD 0114

TABLE OF CONTENTS

PREFACE
FREEING THE RUNNER WITHIN: YOUR CRUCIAL FIRST STEP
BY T.J. MURPHY

NFL football players, elite military athletes, fighter pilots, San Francisco Ballet dancers, Tour de France cyclists, world-class CrossFitters and powerlifters, and runners of all varieties—this is the sort of range of athletes who have benefited from Dr. Kelly Starrett's particular genius when it comes to movement and mechanics.

Kelly's own background is equally eclectic. He was a member of the USA Canoe and Kayak Team and competed in two world championships with the Men's Whitewater Rafting Team. His interests are wide and far-ranging, from surfing to martial arts to skateboarding to Olympic lifting to so-you-think-you-can-dancing.

In a way, Kelly's journey to becoming an internationally renowned expert in movement began at the end of his kayaking career. While putting in yet another hour of hard training—on top of the thousands he had already logged—his neck and shoulder went into a human version of a computer crashing. He couldn't turn his head. His professional whitewater career was done.

That's when his obsession with movement and mechanics began. Spend some time with Kelly, and you become distinctly aware that he sees and processes everything through a 300x lens. As his wife, Juliet Starrett, once told me, Kelly can sense illness and injury in others before any symptoms have manifested. It was natural that he gravitated toward becoming a doctor of physical therapy, and later becoming an innovative thinker in performance-related solutions at the internationally regarded Stone Clinic in San Francisco.

One day, while practicing a series of combat moves with a knife that he saw in a video on the Internet, Kelly stumbled upon CrossFit, the then-fledgling fitness program based on constantly varying functional movements performed at high intensity. Soon enough, he and Juliet opened up one of the first CrossFit affiliates in the world, San Francisco CrossFit. His physical therapy insight and knowledge, let loose within the lab-like environment that is a CrossFit gym, enabled him to observe and learn from the many thousands of workouts through which he coached his gym's members. It spawned an electrically charged new line of thinking about how to solve the various problems that crop up in regard to athletic performance.

This book is about running. Distance running, yes, but also the problems that *all* athletes who run face—from those just beginning in fitness to the professional NFL cornerback who runs as a player and also in training. It's for CrossFit athletes— many of whom make it clear that they "hate" running—and for experienced ultramarathoners who are sick of being mired in injuries.

The ideas and framework that Kelly sets forth in this book are not just about preventing and dealing with injuries. A tremendous bonus to solving injury-related problems with solutions based on mechanics, position, and mobility is that it also frees up extra performance that you may not have known you had. The same tissue restrictions that are causing your knee pain may also be robbing you of some hidden flow of power output. By improving the positions you adopt and the health of the tissues involved and installing normal range of motion in your joints, you may find additional energy to help you run faster and longer.

By improving the positions you adopt and the health of the tissues involved and installing normal range of motion in your joints, you may find additional energy to help you run faster and longer.

In my case, opening my mind to Kelly's ideas was not just about solving a nagging injury. It was about solving *all* of my nagging injuries—including one that, as I can see looking back, was similar to what Kelly experienced on his last day as a professional kayaker.

It was November 2011, and I was staying in a Midtown hotel in New York City. I was five weeks away from running a half-marathon in Las Vegas. It was a Saturday, and my training plan called for a tempo run of 4.5 miles at a pace where I would average 170 to 175 heartbeats per minute.

As I prepared to knock out the run on a treadmill in the hotel gym, I didn't have a clue how much this single workout would impact the direction of my life as an athlete and a runner.

My goal for the half-marathon was not time-specific. Rather, it was to log an uninterrupted year of consistent training, a feat that had eluded my grasp for more than a decade. It was a clear-cut, blue-collar task, like polishing off a year of work as a truck driver—nothing fancy about it. Yet it was as if I was driving the truck on a road riven into shards of rock. When I started training in 2011, I dared to look back at the wreckage of the preceding years of struggling to maintain my identity as an athlete. On rare occasions I was able to hold it together long enough to earn a marathon or Ironman finisher's T-shirt, but I would pay dearly after such efforts, moving through life as if I had jumped through the windshield of my truck and effectively run over myself.

In my 40s, my injuries ran wild. I was like a scene from *The Evil Dead.* Stabbing chronic knee pains and a trick back upended whatever running goal I was limping my way toward. These stoppages and their inherent psychological free falls came with the added drag of getting fat. When I was at my fastest as a runner, I weighed 160 to 165 pounds. After one of my injury forays, my weight floated up toward 210. Which made my next attempt at defying the pattern of chronic injury all the harder.

It is painfully embarrassing to recount the debilitating injuries I stacked one on top of the other for so many years.

I'm like a lot of folks who run or play sports that involve running: I do it for the fresh air and sanity that it delivers. I am inspired by the 70-, 80-, and 90-somethings who refuse to retire themselves to full-time spectator status. I've watched an 80-year-old finish an Ironman triathlon—2.4 miles of swimming, 112 miles of biking, and 26.2 miles of running—in under 17 hours. I talked to a 60-year-old German triathlete over the phone who had completed an Ironman in under 10 hours.

On weekends, I walk my dog near a field where a crowd of athletes who are around 60 years old play soccer, and just the other day, while at the CrossFit Games, I saw a video featuring a CrossFitter who was 100 years old.

For more and more people of all ages and backgrounds, being an athlete is at least as important as cheering for the stars who play on a favorite big-league team. I love watching a good football game, but I find participating in the local Turkey Trot more satisfying than watching the Super Bowl. (A great Super Bowl Sunday for me is one where I do a race in the morning and then watch the game in the afternoon.) I'd argue that being able to think of yourself as an athlete is more vital than having season tickets to anything.

Over the years, I've spoken with scores of former couch potatoes who were transformed by a first triathlon or first CrossFit workout. One quick example: A woman who has since become a good friend of mine, Irene Mejia, weighed 400 pounds when she started CrossFit. Her self-image was 1,000 light-years away from any thoughts of being an athlete. She could barely walk, let alone run.

Now, Irene has slashed that weight almost in half. She trains, she runs, and she competes in CrossFit-style competitions. As another friend put it, "Becoming an athlete saved her life."

Running well is integral to many sports.[1] Running fast, running a lot, and being able to do so without collecting chronic injury problems is crucial to being able to train and compete. Whether running itself is your thing, or whether you run to train for a sport, or whether running is a key part of your sport, running is (as discussed in Chapter 2) part of the fabric of being a human being—especially a modern human being who pursues the likes of soccer, basketball, track and field, or CrossFit. For first responders in the military, law enforcement, and firefighting worlds, being able to run (often under load and in extreme circumstances) is vital to saving lives.

Recreational distance running, by the way, is booming. According to the 2013 National Runner Survey, most of us run to stay healthy, have fun, and burn off stress. The ritual of running is a form of meditation for many of the 30 million Americans identified by the Sport & Fitness Association as "core participant" runners. Yet it's also a competitive challenge: In 2013, 541,000 people finished a marathon in the United States, a country that hosts some 1,100 opportunities to complete the classic 26.2-mile distance. The running boom of the 1970s continues to this day: More women are running, more Masters runners are competing, and a record amount of money is being spent on gear, with expectations that in the coming years nearly $4 billion will be spent annually on shoes alone.

So when injuries steal running away from you, it can hit you hard. Again, I'm not atypical of American runners. Surveys and research suggest that approximately three out of four runners get at least one running-related injury per year. For those runners training for a marathon, 90 percent struggle with some form of ailment in the process.

And it's not just pure runners who become afflicted by these types of overuse injuries. In a recent interview, Dr. Nicolas Romanov, a famed sports scientist and an expert

[1] It's not necessary, however. In fact, two of the most impressive athletes I have had the privilege of writing about are David Bailey and Carlos Moleda. Bailey was a motocross superstar who was paralyzed in an accident on a jump; Moleda a Navy SEAL who was shot and paralyzed during the U.S. operation to remove Noriega from power in 1989. They became competitors in the challenged-athlete division of the Hawaii Ironman, recording one of the greatest rivalries in the history of multisport.

on running and human movement, told me that data being collected in the soccer world is equally alarming. "The players spend tremendous amounts of time refining their soccer skills, but not their running skills," he said. He went on to tell me that in his analysis of soccer players, very few run well. Running is left to chance, and injuries swoop in and bite hard.

Romanov had the same thing to say about elite CrossFit athletes. Although technique is emphasized in the Olympic lifting and gymnastics elements of this fitness discipline, he sees few CrossFitters who run with good form. "They have all the strength they could ever possibly need to run well," he told me. "They just don't put any thought into their running positions and mechanics." This lack of attention, he added, puts even the most powerful athletes at risk for injury when they do an interval workout or a distance run.

In 2011, I was on the brink. I had simply decided to bulldoze my way through any injury or hint of injury. I stretched, did a core strength routine, and practiced the most vigilant and restrictive diet I could think of, going vegan. I spent hundreds of dollars on motion-control shoes and high-end arch supports. When injuries did stir, I opted to complete my workouts on a treadmill, figuring that the reduction in pounding would help.

Which is why I was doing my run on the hotel treadmill in New York. The day before, while walking in the city, my right knee had begun collapsing on me. My many years of experience with running injuries hadn't prepared me for this weird iteration of a funky knee problem. I would walk three or four steps and then it would just buckle, as if the joint was a hinge and someone was sneakily pulling the pin on me.

It was a bad enough problem that each time my knee gave out, I attracted an assortment of concerned looks from my fellow pedestrians.

I hoped that it was a temporary glitch that would evaporate like a bad dream. But it never did. Rather, the condition of my knee degraded as the day wore on. That night, I spent $70 on knee braces, ice bags, and monster bottle of Advil at a Duane Reade. I turned my hotel room into an impromptu medical tent.

The next day, I prepared for the tempo run by wrapping my knee with an Ace bandage and then buckling on the knee brace I'd bought. A handful of Advil had been digested, and the anti-inflammatory chemicals were whizzing through my circulatory system.

Repressing all the capacity I had for rational judgment, I discovered that if I focused my attention on landing my foot at a certain angle, I could keep the mysterious knee-collapsing pattern at bay. This tactic worked well enough that I was able to pull off the entire tempo run. I felt incredible relief as I iced the knee following the workout.

Thanks to what I've learned from Kelly, I now understand that my misguided treadmill workout was the final cost in a long series of charges, and it was time to pay. There would be no more running in 2011. Despite my consultations with sports medicine clinicians and my manic interventions with massage therapy and anti-inflammatories, my leg had gone on strike. Some inner mechanism of evolutionary wisdom encoded into my brain shut me down, saying, "Your authority over the guidance and usage of the right leg has been rescinded until further notice." My goal to complete a year of consistent training was a shambles.

I've had a few years to reflect on my fevered state of mind in late 2011, when I felt that injury was a natural by-product of being a runner. Injuries were meant to be avoided if possible through the right choice of running shoes, but otherwise, you just ran through them as best you could. Injuries were the enemy, and it was a mind-over-matter thing.

It never dawned on me that my vigorous denial and reliance on over-the-counter interventions might be flawed. It also never occurred to me that the injuries were manifestations of weak spots in my personal infrastructure and the way I ran. A deeper look into the root cause of each and every injury would have uncovered a hole or weakness that—if corrected—would have offered me not just a pain-free running experience, but also more performance: more speed, more endurance, and faster race times recorded with less energy burned.

I was incredibly lucky to have been talking with the founder of CrossFit Endurance, ultrarunner Brian MacKenzie, who helped open my mind to a new way of thinking about running, being a runner, and the role of injury. Because if I had stayed the course and tried to do another power-sweep through 2012 the way I had through 2011, I almost certainly would have ended up having a knee or hip replaced or an Achilles tendon surgically repaired.

MacKenzie teaches an innovative approach that integrates running technique, strength and conditioning, and nutrition into a low-mileage/high-performance/low-injury world of distance running that I never could have imagined. As my blood loyalty to traditional methods of distance running finally eased, I listened to what MacKenzie was saying. After considering the depth and breadth of my injury problems, the first thing he said to me was, "You need to see Kelly Starrett."

A few weeks later I met with Kelly, who is a doctor of physical therapy, and was set on a new path. My knee—which had continued to buckle on me every few steps for weeks— quickly found a new life of stability. Since the day I met Kelly, I haven't limped. I also was set on a journey that has allowed me to return to a full embrace of running that feels almost bulletproof. The ideas, practices, and techniques that he put forth to me and countless other runners who have moved through the world of the MobilityWOD have been sharpened and distilled into the pages of the book you now hold in your hands.

It enabled me to once again live the athlete's life.

But it's my contention that a new generation of leaders in the running world—like Kelly Starrett, Brian MacKenzie, Nicholas Romanov, a running podiatrist named Nick Campitelli, and *Born to Run* author Christopher McDougall—have an underlying message that is finally breaking through and driving a new era in running forward. This message is not merely a list of programming ideas and techniques. It's much more vast and cogent.

In Kelly's case, it's the main thrust of his position, and it's the first thing you read when you log onto MobilityWOD.com, the website he co-founded with his wife, Juliet:

"All human beings should be able to perform basic maintenance on themselves."

He says that although we may not think we have a choice, we do. If you like running and hate being injured, you can take matters into your own hands and fundamentally shut the door on the chronic injuries that drive you nuts.

What if you can't even begin to imagine that you are a runner? Running either seems too inaccessible or too ridden with pain, or you have been led to believe that you were born with flat feet or bad knees and that running is for others, not for you. Whether it's running in a 10k or rattling off a quarter-mile repeat in a CrossFit workout, somewhere along the line you have been told or have come to the conclusion that running is too damaging for you.

To unbind yourself from this thinking, it begins with understanding that "All human beings should be able to perform basic maintenance on themselves." It's not a magic pill, but it is a path of thinking and working that holds within it the promise that you can free the athlete within.

It's simple, but it's not easy, and the first thing you have to let go of is the belief that all you have to do (or all you *can* do) is hand your credit card to a physical therapist, a podiatrist, or a salesperson at a running shoe store and expect someone else to fix the problem. Being Ready to Run requires your attention and work.

There's no magical cure. In fact, what the raging debate about minimalist shoes versus traditional running shoes has exposed is that the debate is asking the wrong question. When it comes to running injuries, the elephant in the room is that shoes aren't the fix. Decades of running shoe technology have failed to slow the rate of injury among runners.

The shoe itself is not going to cure your ails, whether it's a minimalist shoe or a 16-ounce motion-control shoe. Same goes for orthotics, muscle stim, ultrasound, heel lifts, knee supports, and the thousands of dollars you can easily sink into the sports medicine industrial complex. The real game-changer is the attitude you and I adopt in our lives as runners: the conviction that we are responsible for taking care of our running machines like a master mechanic would. As Chris McDougall has said in response to *Born to Run* critics—the ones who read the book and rushed off to buy a pair of minimalist running shoes expecting that they would instantly be transformed into barefoot runners, only to get injured within a matter of days or weeks—they missed the point. Yes, you can reclaim the natural running capacities that you were born with, but you've got to do the work. Smart, patient, consistent work. If you are looking for a magic pill in a running shoe—or any other intervention, for that matter— you're doomed to the treadmill of injury, with the prospect that you will one day wear something out for real.

This is both the challenge and the promise of this book for those who want to be able to run well and run often until the end of their days. You are born to run. Although modern living, poor running form, muscular imbalances, and being stubborn enough to think that you can run through injuries like a tank through a field of saplings (the latter being one I'm particularly guilty of) may have set you back, there is

The real game-changer is the attitude we adopt in our lives as runners: the conviction that we are responsible for taking care of our running machines like a master mechanic would.

a reset button that you can push. It all starts with taking responsibility, plotting a course of action, and being patient, thorough, and persistent in seeing it done today, tomorrow, and forever after.

Kelly Starrett's mindset and approach are meant to be the bridge. If you want to unleash all the power and endurance that your body was indeed born with, *Ready to Run* will help get you there.

INTRODUCTION

A TYPICAL DAY IN
THE LIFE OF A RUNNER

You are a full court press runner, and this is what it looks like:

After six, maybe seven hours of sleep, the alarm goes off at 4:30. It's dark, it's cold, it's Wednesday. The Earth is whirling rapidly on its axis. Tasks in your immediate future include preparing an eight-year-old for school: getting up, getting dressed, preparing breakfast, and packing the backpack, including homework and lunch, plus delivering her safely to the cul-de-sac of the elementary school. You also need to wedge in time for one last rehearsal of a PowerPoint presentation you will be giving at 9:00, and there's a 40-minute drive-time commute to be negotiated.

But first, you want to squeeze in your daily run. Either you run now in the pre-dawn, or it's just not going to happen. The morning run is a task—and despite any lingering soreness or nagging pains, your mind is set with unbendable intent. When it comes to the completion of this task, you will not be denied.

So you're awake at 4:30, and it's dark, and freezing rain is falling at a steep slant. You step from the bed into a pair of flip-flops with arch supports in them so that you don't put any undue pressure on your always-touchy arches.

You assimilate appropriate weather-resistant attire, throw back an Americano, and you're out the door. During the first mile and a half, you feel all the usual hotspots flare: that pinch of pain just below your right kneecap, the swelling in the bone of your right heel, the nervy sketchiness deep in the socket of your left hip. You have invested considerable American Express capacity toward a variety of measures meant to dull these various stings: Over-the-counter orthotics planted in $150 motion-control shoes. A neoprene and rubber tourniquet strapped just below the knee that came with the following promise: Don't let tendinitis, cartilage wear, or chondromalacia stop your training!

The pains simmer down, and you knock out the rest of the 5-miler. If you can carve out a minute of time, you kick up a foot onto a park bench, try to touch your toes, and spend 20 seconds or so doing what you think of as a hamstring stretch. You get back to the house in time to begin the rest of the morning adventure. The 5 miles of the week's 45 are logged. You remain on course for your upcoming race.

After delivering your presentation, you repair to your office, sit down at your computer, and begin motoring through work. In your dress shoes are a different pair of arch supports with an extra few millimeters of heel lift to take the edge off the soreness in your Achilles tendon. When you walk, your feet angle outward and cave in, and your knees follow in a subtle yet degenerative way, cementing the pattern of your current foot strike, one that chews away at the soft tissues around your knees. The arch supports are supposed to defray this problem as well. Then there's your back: You've thought about getting some sort of lumbar support to attach to your work chair to help buffer that always-lurking sciatica pain that has started shooting through your hips and threatens to bring your running to a halt. In a drawer of your desk is a bottle holding nearly 100 coated gel caplets, each spring-loaded with 200 milligrams of ibuprofen.

Take a moment to appreciate the dedication involved here. You may not be an Olympian, but tell me that there isn't an Olympian's drive at work in powering through a day like this, week in, week out, month after month, year after year.

The only thing that will slow you down? Or stop you? If you're like nearly 80 percent of runners, an injury is going to force you to stop at some point in the year (and you're at even more risk if you heel-strike, or land on your heel as opposed to your mid-foot or forefoot, when you run). Rather than lacing up a pair of shoes, you'll be cinching up an AquaJogger or strapping your feet into the pedals of a Lifecycle.

Here's the thing: The human body is an amazing, adaptable, nearly unstoppable survival machine designed to absorb the wear-and-tear of millions of duty cycles. The above example demonstrates how the body can absorb a tremendous amount of damage before serving up the kind of injury that forces a complete stop.

Living through that kind of daily schedule is only adding to the wear-and-tear caused by the daily run. The tissues are dehydrated, like beef jerky, and are not given adequate time to warm up. The shoes are enabling a heel strike that increases the forces of shear and the amount of impact stress on the body—it's like driving a Ferrari with the hand brake on.

But what if I were to tell you that there is another way? This routine requires an impressive amount of self-discipline and desire. What if you channeled some of that energy into several small, new habits that produce two types of results?

- **Improved performance**
- **Reduced risk of injury**

In *Ready to Run*, I want you to explore a new way of thinking about those signal flares that the various tissues and structures of your body send up. If you find yourself

The human body is an amazing, adaptable, nearly unstoppable survival machine designed to absorb the wear-and-tear of millions of duty cycles.

trying to bury nagging chronic injury pain through common interventions, like new shoes, inserts, ice, and ibuprofen, I want you to find a new appreciation for the signals you're receiving from your body, whether it's arch pain, back pain, a dull ache in your hamstring, or a sharp pain under your knee. Each of these signals is a clue to how you can unleash more performance. By solving the underlying problem, you will not only extinguish the pain and prevent the injury that is rising to the surface, but also gain an additional measure of speed, power, or efficiency—and likely a combination of those three elements.

A BETTER DAY

Let's reconsider how you might approach that morning routine by looking through this alternate lens:

You get up at 4:30 and, in addition to or instead of a cup of coffee, you down 16 ounces of water mixed with an electrolyte enhancer like Osmo or Nuun. As always, you walk about the house barefoot. While you drink your water/electrolyte solution to help restore the water you lost while sleeping, you perform a brief mobility drill to open up your hip extension and unglue the sliding surfaces around your heel cords.

If your training schedule calls for a run or a workout that includes running, instead of wearing an overbuilt motion-control running shoe that shortens your heel cord and acts like a cast, you have progressed to a flat, zero-drop running shoe that enables your foot to work like a foot.

You spend the first part of your running workout performing a CrossFit Endurance–style warm-up, mixing 100-meter runs and dynamic movements with 100-meter jogs to engage and warm up the muscles and connective tissues that will be called upon for the workout. Then, thoroughly warmed up and hot, with the juices flowing, you launch into your run for the day (or CrossFit workout, or basketball practice—whatever your athletic discipline that includes running).

You spend the last part of your running workout warming down with something as simple as a five-minute walk. This assists your lymphatic system in doing the job of removing wastes from the interstitial fluids surrounding the muscles and connective tissues that just propelled you through your workout.

Later, at the office, you try to sit as little as possible so as not to shut off your lymphatic system or shorten the muscles that support a neutral spine position. When you stand and walk, you monitor the position of your feet—they are straight—and maintain a light engagement of the muscles of your butt and core to set your pelvis and spine in a neutral position. When you do have to sit, you remain especially aware of maintaining a neutral posture. You have also built in the habit of blending in short mobility drills every hour or two to fix your feet, improve your spinal position, and work the areas above and below any missing bits of motor control and range of motion that are impeding your performance and adding to your risk of injury. You eat a nutritious diet, you hydrate with electrolyte fluids, and you have added compression socks to your work wardrobe to again help open up the pipes so that your lymphatic system replaces waste products with nutrient flow.

You've dumped the Advil. Replacing it in your desk drawer is a bicycle tube so that you can zap inflammation with a bout of VooDoo Floss Band compression.

At night, you dedicate 10 minutes to the effort of ferreting out any warning signs that your body may be sending you— nagging signals that you treat not as fires to be stamped out, but as problems to be solved, with fresh performance to be gained as a result. It's not about just getting in some stretching. Your worldview of solving athletic dysfunction problems has expanded far beyond the simple and ineffectual hamstring

You are on a mission to correct missing range of motion problems and poor movement patterns.

stretch. Rather, you are on a mission to correct missing range of motion problems and poor movement patterns—you know that any weaknesses in motor control and range of motion are opportunities to inject a solid performance boost into your running.

NO MAGIC PILL

This isn't a stretching book. It's a book for the Formula 1 runner seeking health and high performance over a lifetime. All human beings should be able *and willing* to perform basic maintenance on themselves. Sports medicine has its place, but you have both a right and a responsibility to know what's going on in your body, take care of as much business as you can, and harvest any performance that's hiding in the shadows.

Which gets to the "why" of this book. Running is a part of your athletic lifestyle. But there's a fatal flaw in the running universe, and it has to do with a decision-making flowchart loop that runners everywhere put to use.

Have you ever experienced the following sequence of problems, thoughts, and actions?

1. You go for a run.
2. After the run, you notice a piercing pain in the usual hotspots: knee, ankle, hip, back.
3. You ice and stretch, but at the end of the day the pain is still there.
4. The next day, hoping that it was all a bad dream, you lace up your shoes and head out the door for a 4-mile test jog.
5. It hurts during first mile. You say a short, impassioned prayer to the running gods to make this bad dream go away. You stop by a tree, try to stretch it out, and then continue.

6. Halfway through, you decide to either walk back or finish the run despite hobbling pain that is worsening.

7. While walking back, you think, "I guess I need a new shoe." It could mean selecting a different model of shoe or replacing a worn-out shoe. You hope that if you visit a shoe store, the problem will vanish with the swipe of a credit card.

This kind of thinking is the fatal flaw: It's not about the shoe. It never was, and it never will be.

When it comes to preventing injuries, the shoe is like the bumper on a car. It offers a layer of protection from the pavement. But when it comes to preventing the intrinsic injuries that are chronic and due to poor mechanics, shoes are not the key to the equation.

It's not about the shoe. It never was, and it never will be. It's about you.

What leads to this flawed thinking may be the magic pill idea. You have a problem that needs to be solved, and it would be great if you could just walk into a store, give your credit card a brief workout, and have it all done with. This same appeal can be found in visits to sports medicine clinics, massage therapists, and the like. While these services can be exceptionally valuable in your life as an athlete, it's the good physiotherapists who give you the upfront, hard truth that the solution cannot be comprised of a shoe and an orthotic. It's not about the shoes.

What's it about? It's about the power you have to make real and lasting change that has the added value of helping you prevent injury as well as uncork new streams of performance.

It's not about the shoes. It's about *you*.

READY TO RUN

What does it mean to be Ready to Run? Whether you're the classic type-A runner I described earlier, or whether running is a part of your sport or your job, I want you to embrace a sort of system check that will inform you on how well tuned your body and your lifestyle are for the various stresses that running places on you. In meeting all of the standards outlined in Part 2 of this book, or at least moving the needle as close as you can to these standards, you will gain confidence that you're optimizing power and minimizing injury risk. The standards are related to your shoes, your physical readiness, your ability to use good positions, your efforts to prepare and recover from training sessions, and the lifestyle choices that affect your overall health and physical condition.

If you are Ready to Run, you have the following things going for you:

- **You have developed a habit of drinking more than 100 ounces of electrolyte-enhanced water each day, thereby ensuring that your tissues are properly hydrated and healthy.**
- **You have a normal amount of hip extension, a key to enabling optimal hip function for more power, more performance, and better mechanics throughout your musculoskeletal system.**
- **You are free of hotspots because, as a part of your ongoing attention to maintenance, you no longer try to run through small, nagging injuries, but rather consider them as signals that you need to improve your positions, mechanics, and tissue health.**

There's plenty more—there are 12 standards. My first mission is to give you a detailed look at each standard to explain what it is and why it's important. After that, I'll go into how to improve your performance in the standards, arming you with an array of mobility exercises that—when performed on a consistent basis—will effect positive change and help you become as Ready to Run as possible.

PART 1

Have you ever asked your physician what to do about an irritating knee or foot problem and received the following two-word prescription: "Stop running"?

Or maybe you're a longtime distance runner who's collected a shoebox full of marathon finisher medals, and you've become so mired in chronic injuries that you're thinking it's time to take up cycling. Or you're convinced that you just weren't born to be a runner. I used to think this way. As a teen, I was an all-around athlete, but the farthest I could run without my knee hurting was 100 yards. I was convinced that I was born to do many things, but running was not one of them. Does that sound familiar? Maybe you think you don't have the right feet, or your knees are shot, or you just don't have the right body for running. So you've avoided running (to the best of your ability) as either a sport or a training mode. For example, you're a CrossFitter who can deadlift 500 pounds easily, but when a workout calls for hard intervals, you brace yourself for a spirit-breaking day or avoid the session altogether.

In the process of becoming a coach and a physical therapist and developing an obsession with the physics of movement, position, and mechanics, I realized that we are all designed to be lifelong runners. We may have to put in some work to reset ourselves, but the path is clear.

In my case, at 230 pounds, I was able to run the Quad Dipsea ultramarathon in a pair of 5-ounce flat shoes. How? It starts with unlearning some things. This is the first step in being Ready to Run.

CHAPTER 1
THE DURABLE RUNNER

Would you like to get all the running mileage that your body was designed to put out?

It starts at the top, with the Olympic marathon, and with imagery that tends to endure longer than that of the first athlete breaking the tape or setting a new world record. In 1968, John Stephen Akhwari of Tanzania limped into the Olympic stadium with strands of athletic tape wrapped around his right knee. He was last, finishing an hour after the winner. The visual of mind-over-body-at-all-costs inspired one journalist to say that it was "a performance that gives meaning to the word courage."

In the 1984 Olympics, Swiss runner Gabriele Andersen-Schiess entered the Olympic stadium some twenty minutes after gold medalist Joan Benoit. Charlie Lovett captures the scene quite well in his book *Olympic Marathon*:

> "The crowd gasped in horror as she staggered onto the track, her torso twisted, her left arm limp, her right leg mostly seized. She waved away medical personnel who rushed to help her, knowing that, if they touched her, she would be disqualified. The L.A. Coliseum crowd applauded and cheered as she limped around the track in the race's final 400 meters, occasionally stopping and holding her head."[2]

[2] Charlie Lovett, *The Olympic Marathon: A Centennial History of the Games' Most Storied Race* (Westport, CT: Praeger Publishers, 1997).

He also could have mentioned that her knee were horribly valgus, collapsing inward with each foot strike, the soft-tissue friction almost shooting sparks. She did all this for thirty-seventh place.

The cheering from the crowd was so loud that Anderson-Schiess—despite the fact that her body was shutting down in front of the approving audience that packed the Coliseum—tried to dig up enough motor control to stick her fingers in her ears.

The image of a broken-down runner finishing an epic endurance race despite any and all physical costs has become part of the ethos of the marathon world. Bent, twisted, and limping, with his wet-tissue systems fried and compromised, he waves off help, crosses the line, and becomes the hero of the day.

The Olympics is the Olympics, and there's a lot to be said about sacrifice and the Olympic Games, but the fact that this task-completion mentality trickles down through the running world is cause for alarm, or at least discussion. There were 541,000 marathon finishers in the United States in 2013.[3] Go spend an hour at the finish after the four-hour finishers have received their medals. Watch the mechanics, the limping, the braces, and the K tape being used to get some of these folks across the line.

Courage is a fantastic thing. I'm all about courage. But when that courage is deployed to force an unprepared or otherwise compromised human body over the 33,000 steps required for a marathon, we should be honest about the costs involved.

What's tremendous about runners is their task-completion mindset. It can also be their undoing.

[3] Running USA Annual Marathon Report, 2014.

110 YEARS

Consider for a moment the life of a Major League Baseball player—perhaps a pitcher with a 95 mph fastball. As Tom Verducci wrote in *Sports Illustrated*:

> "Walk into any major league clubhouse before a game and you will see all kinds of strength trainers, masseuses, massage therapists, doctors, whirlpools, hydrotherapy pools, hot tubs, cold tubs, weight rooms, gyms…and injured pitchers."[4]

[4] Tom Verducci, "With More Closers Breaking Down, It's Time to Rethink the Modern Bullpen," *Sports Illustrated*, April 17, 2012.

If you're a starting pitcher playing 35 games a year and you have a long career in the majors (being a pitcher and having a long career in the majors tend to be mutually exclusive), you likely will trash your shoulder and elbow more than a few dozen times over. Let's say you retire at age 30 and, thanks to the ceaseless grind of a high-powered repetitive motion, you've worn out something for real.

If you were making $10 million a year or more, that experience probably goes down in the books fairly well. You gave your arm to baseball and were well compensated for it.

But a runner? This is what I want you to think about. If you have any of these three performance-sucking problems (and they tend to come as a set), then you're accelerating the burn rate of your joints and soft tissues each time your foot strikes the ground:

- **Poor positions**
- **Restricted range of motion**
- **Habitual poor movement patterns**

Although your body is designed to last you 110 years, you can shred through it in 20 if you try hard enough.

If you have a multimillion-dollar contract in place, there may be room for debate. But if you're running for the sheer love of it…what then?

The human body is an amazing and adaptable machine that jumps when you tell it to jump, through all sorts of past injuries and new injuries that may be rising to the surface. When the mind says yes, the body obeys. Until it comes to a smoking halt.

There's a cost, and the cost is this: If you want to enjoy being a runner for as many of those years as possible—and when I say "enjoy," I also mean to tap into all the speed, power, and endurance that your amazing machine has to offer—then it's your job to support the task-completion ethos with another ethos:

If you're going to make the demands on your body that being an athlete requires, then it's your job to support that body.

Supporting your body means constantly working toward installing and maintaining the following practices:

- **Habitually seeking optimal positions from which to transmit power**
- **Developing the movement systems of your body so that they have access to the full ranges of motion that your body was designed to have**
- **Practicing and mastering good movement patterns and positions**
- **Developing the strength and conditioning to support good movement patterns from the first mile to the twenty-sixth and beyond**

If you've suffered an injury that requires a visit to the primary care doctor listed on your health insurance policy, you likely know the drill: You can see from the shoes she's wearing that she's not a runner, so you see it coming fast, that moment after she assesses your Achilles tendinopathy or patella tendinitis and then looks you in the eye as if you should not have left the mental hospital earlier than scheduled, because the antidote is as obvious as the smell of the exam room disinfectant.

"Stop running," she says.

That's not me. I'm on your side. I want you to run today, I want you to run well, I want you to improve, and someday, when the time comes, I want you to be the badass at the all-comers track meet who is the only one in the 90-to-95-year-old age group to report to the starting line for the 400 meters.

Consider this book an owner's manual for the high-performance runner-for-life.

KEY PRINCIPLES

To get started, I want you to think about the key principles on which the *Ready to Run* approach is based.

It's about performance

When you think of injury prevention, you probably think of those techniques recommended in magazine articles that are supposed to reduce ankle pronation or soften the impact of your foot strike. This usually entails using orthotics and running less on the pavement and more on the golf course. But these techniques are like Band-Aids that only help stall the inevitable.

What I'm after in this book is to motivate and guide you toward the attainment of 12 clear and measurable standards that will hit the reset button on how you move and how you think about movement. The payoff from doing the work to achieve and maintain these standards is more than reducing your risk of injury, and more than putting a stop to wearing out your joints. When you fix problems and retrain your body to move well, you also allow for greater performance—more power, more speed, and you'll be able to hold it together longer, too. You will reduce the risk of injuries, yes, but in the process you'll also get better.

Alter the task-completion mindset

It's great that you have the discipline to climb out of bed at 4:30 in the morning and check your daily run off the list before the first hint of dawn. That's fantastic. But I want more from you. I'm asking you to go the extra mile and hold the quality of your running to a higher standard. That means asking yourself these kinds of questions:

- How well do you run each mile?
- Do you warm up your systems and tissues before you run?
- Do you hydrate?
- Do you cool down?
- Do you spend the bulk of your day standing, moving, and sitting with an awareness of the quality of your positions and mechanics?
- Do you counter any lousy movement patterns with an appropriate dose of maintenance work?

It's great that you are steadfast and consistent with your training. But in taking your dedication to another level, you will get the most out of each and every training session.

Take personal responsibility for routine maintenance

So you're a runner, and a busy one at that—so busy that you wish to farm out injury prevention and rehab to professionals. Let them worry about it, in other words. Well, the sports medicine industrial complex is happy to take this task off your shoulders and help you lighten up your wallet at the same time. Sure, there are times when you need a doctor or physiotherapist to help you work through problems and make decisions. But the hard truth is that routine maintenance on your personal running machine can be and should be performed *by you.*

This is a bedrock principle within this book, and it is the primary directive of my teaching. When it comes to this running machine, you can change the oil and inflate the tires. I know you're busy, I know your day is crammed, and I know you have a boss and a spouse and your kid's science fair project to help out with. That's why, when it comes to routine maintenance, I'm asking for just 10 minutes a day.

Routine maintenance on your personal running machine can be and should be performed by you.

No days off

I'm asking for just 10 minutes a day for maintenance work, but you need to put in those 10 minutes *every day.* No days off, no excuses.

It's a learning process that never ends

The path I am offering here will help you solve problems and set your running free. Each problem you solve will help you tap into the athletic potential that's been hidden in the shadows. But new problems will crop up. This is a part of your new mindset. In the old task-completion model, aches and pains that begin to stir are annoyances to be plowed over with a hamstring stretch and a bag of ice. The new model suggests a different attitude: When you find a new problem to solve, rather than turn on the ignition in the bulldozer or sink into despair, I want you to embrace it.

Problems are going to keep coming. Each one is a gift waiting to be opened—some new area of performance you didn't know you had, or some new efficiency to be gained. The 90- to 95-year-old division of the Masters Track and Field Nationals awaits. A lifelong commitment to solving each problem that creeps up is the ticket.

Mobilizing replaces stretching

Two minutes of half-assed stretching can do a tight muscle more harm than good. Think about what would happen if you took your favorite T-shirt, grabbed it at two ends, and gave it a good, long, static stretch. You would get a thinned-out, stretched-out T-shirt for your efforts. With that image in mind, think of your muscle tissue. If you manage to stretch it out and lengthen it and then launch into a hard run, do you think that you have the strength, conditioning, and specific coordination to support the change in this variable? How does changing this one variable work within the long equation that is the biological symphony of running? It's a gamble. Starting now, take haphazard end-range muscle stretching out of your routine and replace it with the intention of improving your range of motion as a system—from how each joint sits in its socket, to the health of your tissues and sliding surfaces, to your motor patterns. This mobilization approach is applied throughout the *Ready to Run* program.

I'm all about courage, hard work, and getting things done. But let's reframe the conversation when it comes to getting all the mileage that your human machine was engineered to deliver.

CHAPTER 2
BORN TO RUN

You run in races, or you run intervals during metabolic conditioning ("MetCon") workouts, or you run within your sport or on the battlefield in the service of your country. Or you want to be running in one of these domains, but you have felt that you just don't have what it takes.

You have what it takes. You have the design and the circuitry to run like the warrior-hunter-gatherer you are.

You may not think that you can run, or that you can run well, but if you reverse-engineer your body, there is only one conclusion to be drawn: Like the Terminator was designed to kill, as a human being you were designed to run. As Christopher McDougall describes our ancestors in his book *Born to Run,* running was hardwired in such a way that it was indispensable to survival:

> "It was the way we thrived and spread across the planet. You ran to eat and to avoid being eaten; you ran to find a mate and impress her, and with her you ran off to start a new life together. You had to love running, or you wouldn't live to love anything else."[5]

[5] Christopher McDougall, *Born to Run* (New York: Random House, 2011).

SURVIVAL OF THE SWIFTEST

It's two million years ago. Do you know where your ancestors are?

Back in the early Pleistocene, human beings faced a real head-scratcher in trying to get through the day. Lions, tigers, rhinoceroses, and leopards abounded, but it was about 1.4 million years before a lightbulb went off and some hotshot thought to lash together a sharp stone and a stick to make a spear. One way for humans to get a more substantial meal than, say, a handful of grass may have been to stay awake at night and listen in on some tigers ripping apart their prey. At dawn, they ran to the scene to get a handful of what was left. If they were spotted by a 600-pound tiger that could go from 0 to 35 mph in just a few heartbeats, they took off. Maybe they had their lucky club with them and maybe they didn't, but either way, running was likely the best solution.

You really were born Ready to Run.

There was scavenging the leftovers of lions and tigers, but also there was hunting. As Harvard paleoanthropologist Daniel Lieberman and his colleagues have argued, early humans, for whom the best available weapon was a club or a sharp stick, probably had to exercise the few advantages they had over wildebeest and the like. The animals cooled themselves by panting and your ancestors could sweat, so even though wildebeests could outsprint the early human hunter, they couldn't outlast him—not while galloping along for hours on a terrifically hot day. The hunter-gatherer loaded with sweat glands would start the chase in the middle of a sunny day and never let the animal get a break under a shady tree. Eventually, the wildebeest, zebra, antelope, or whatever, under relentless pressure from the *Homo erectus* runner-type who could just keep going and going and going, would collapse—hence the phrase "persistence hunting."[6]

[6] Daniel E. Lieberman, *The Story of the Human Body: Evolution, Health, and Disease* (New York: Vintage, 2013).

YOUR RUNNING WEAPONRY

It's not just the gifts of peach-fuzz fur and a superior heat tolerance mechanism. Human beings have an assortment of keen advantages over other mammals when it comes to running. So the next time you hear someone say, "I could never run a marathon—I can't even run around the block!" or you encounter a CrossFitter who has tremendous work capacity and unbridled pain tolerance in the gym but says, "I hate running," here's some evolutionary trivia to respond with:

- **You have springs.** When you walk, your feet, legs, and body use a pendulum-like motion. But shift into a run, and all the miraculous machinery that you were born with vaults into action—your hips, knees, ankles, and feet work in concert with your muscles and connective tissues to use gravity and elastic energy to bounce you along with breathtaking efficiency. "In fact, a running human's legs store and release energy so efficiently that running is only about 30 to 50 percent more costly than walking in the endurance-speed range," says Daniel Lieberman in his book *The Story of the Human Body*. "What's more, these springs are so effective that they can make the cost of endurance running (but not sprinting) independent of speed: it costs the same number of calories to run five miles at a pace of either 7 or 10 minutes per mile."

- **You have stable, springy arches.** Your feet are serious machines designed not only for running, but also for *fast* running—as well as the quick, agile changes of direction that we associate with a star halfback in football. The mechanism that is the human arch, with its energy-returning spring action, helps reduce the energy cost of running by up to 17 percent, according to researchers.[7]

[7] R. F. Ker, M. B. Bennett, S. R. Bibby, R. C. Kester, and R. M. Alexander, "The Spring in the Arch of the Human Foot," *Nature* 325 (1987): 147-49.

- **You have super-elastic Achilles tendons.** Just a third of an inch long in a chimp, the human Achilles tendon is 6 inches long. When you run, you show off the true power of your wondrous heel cords: They can store and release 35 percent of the mechanical energy produced when you run—something that doesn't happen when you walk. The Achilles is all about helping you run.

- **You have a powerful butt.** That's right; your large glute muscles are not there just to fill out a pair of designer jeans. You can walk around with your glutes essentially asleep. Break into a sprint, however, and your butt becomes essential to your overall stability—it keeps you from doing a face plant with every step. The glutes are the largest muscles in your body, and if you put them to full advantage (a life of sitting in chairs can impede on the magnificent flow of power that your posterior chain was engineered to channel), you will be using muscles that are relatively inexhaustible.

- **You have ear canals like spacecraft guidance computers.** Yes, even your ear canals are specialized for good running. Running involves a lot more banging around than walking does—just observe the figure-eight movement of a runner's ponytail in action to get a sense of how much is going on as you bound down the road. Like a computer with gyroscopes, the ear canals transmit signals to your musculoskeletal system to correct for the constant flow of tiny imbalances incurred in a bipedal organism on the move.

If you have any doubts that, thanks to millions of years of evolution, you were born to run—whether you're running on the field, on the court, in your combat boots, or in a marathon—read Lieberman's book *The Story of the Human Body*. There's a reason you have short toes (foot stabilization 101), a narrow waist in contrast to wide shoulders (power generated through optimal rotation), a powerful butt, gyroscopes in your skull, and skin that radiates away excess body heat thanks to millions of sweat glands: You were designed to run like the wind. This book is meant to help you let it rip.

PART 2

The mission of this book is to offer those who run or want to run a clear set of guidelines. Whether you're a distance runner, a soccer player, a CrossFitter, or a soldier, I want to help you make sure that you are ready to be the best runner you can be and to decrease your chances of wear, tear, and injury. The standards that I put forth in this part of the book are designed to help you determine how Ready to Run you are and help you reach the optimal range of capacity that your body was designed to deliver.

CHAPTER 3
INTRODUCTION TO THE STANDARDS

In the following chapters, I introduce and explain the 12 standards that you'll use to complete a thorough assessment of your state of being Ready to Run. They are:

- Neutral feet
- Flat shoes
- A supple thoracic spine
- An efficient squatting technique
- Hip flexion
- Hip extension
- Ankle range of motion
- Warming up and cooling down
- Compression
- No hotspots
- Hydration
- Jumping and landing

Pursuing, achieving, and maintaining these 12 standards produces the following results:

- Your tissues will be healthy and hydrated, and the surfaces between your tissues will slide and glide rather than stick like Velcro.
- Your joints will be in their proper positions.

- Normal range of motion will be restored so that your ankles, knees, and hips work the way they are designed to, unleashing your full power and minimizing the destructive forces that can wear holes in your wheels.
- Essential mechanics and motor control patterns will be reinstalled so that when you stand, walk, and run, you are not chewing up cartilage and connective tissue.
- Your hip function will be optimal, resulting in more power for your running, less stress on your knees, and the capacity to run with good form, whether you're a beginner setting out on your first run or CrossFit workout, or you're a longtime competitive runner heading into the deepest, darkest corners of the fatigue that hits in long runs and races.
- And more.

We all may be born to run, but something often goes awry along the way. Things go pretty well until we have to buckle ourselves into desks in first grade. You see, your tissues and joints mold to the positions in which you spend most of your time. If you spend a significant portion of each day bound to a chair or in shoes that elevate your heels, your body becomes warped and restricted by those patterns. Add to that a good chunk of time spent with your head hunched over your phone as you type texts, and the results can be crippling. These new shapes and tendencies of your tissues and joints are no longer conducive to running. You must now be *re*born to run.

YOU CAN CHANGE

The first step on this path of rebirth is acknowledging that you can restore your natural capacities despite the damage that you may have incurred from too much sitting, too little self-maintenance, and too much reliance on overbuilt running shoes, painkillers, and sheer force of will to burn your way through physical obstacles.

The key premise of this book is that you can change. It starts with the mindset that the key to enjoying running for a lifetime lies within the body itself, and that your job is to pave the way.

What does it take to restore your tissues, joints, and mechanics to optimal levels? The 12 standards are guideposts. They are targets that involve lifestyle, range of motion, movement capacity, and habits related to running.

The standards are presented in a yes-or-no, binary fashion. There is no gray area. The test for each standard will tell you that, yes, on that measure you are ready to run, or no, you have work to do to meet that standard. There is no one-size-fits-all program for achieving the standards, but after you see where you stand on each one, I'll give you tools and strategies for flipping the switch from no to yes.

The key to enjoying running for a lifetime lies within the body itself, and your job is to pave the way.

CHASING THE STANDARDS

Although I'll go into more detail about this later in the book, I want to emphasize here the most important criteria in chasing the standards. Keep these fundamental principles at the forefront of your thinking:

- **Be patient.** A standard may seem impossible to you when you perform the initial test—especially if you have years of running combined with years of sitting in chairs under your belt. First, don't be discouraged. Your tissues have a remarkable capacity to change. If you've been spending hours a day in a chair, your tissues have adapted to that position, which is not a position that allows for powerful hip function. But your body has an elastic quality, and it can change. Just know that it's not going to happen overnight. Eat the elephant one bite at a time, as they say.

Set small goals and knock them out one by one. Commit yourself to the program for the long haul. If you're engaged in chipping away at a standard on a daily basis, you're more than halfway there. Going after it is where the money's at.

- **Be creative.** In Part 3, I offer a basic set of mobilizations to help you attack certain blockages that may be preventing you from achieving a standard. These "mobs," as I call them, will get you started. But ultimately you're in charge. There are multiple paths available, and I want you to think creatively. If you travel by plane a lot and sit in the window seat for five hours or more at a time, for example, go in armed for combat. Bring a rolling pin or softball with you on the plane, wear compression gear, and bring a tube of electrolyte tablets for the water to hydrate. And what about your overall strategy for achieving a challenging range of motion standard? You might ask, "Is it okay to use Pilates to help me achieve the Hip Flexion standard?" Absolutely. You might use Pilates, you might go to CrossFit classes, or you might dig up old Jack Lalanne episodes. Be creative about how you build rituals into your life to seek, achieve, and maintain the standards.

- **Test and retest.** Here's a tactic to get the most out of your investment in this work: Test yourself before and after performing a mobilization. For example, say you're spending two minutes working on ankle range of motion with a specific exercise. Test your range of motion before the exercise, and then test it again afterward. Do you see an improvement? If you've registered a change, great. If not, try a different mobilization or use a different tool—go hunting for the right combination that initiates change in the tissue.

- **Keep after it.** There is no finish line, of course. One of the mantras of the *Ready to Run* program is "No Days Off." Depending on your background, your age, the state of your tissues, and the amount of work you put in, pursuing and maintaining the standards is like pursuing and maintaining good dental health. It's never over. If you're just starting out—as a runner, a CrossFitter, a field-sport athlete, an aspiring soldier, or maybe all of the above—don't let the distance of the journey overwhelm you. By investing 10 minutes a day over weeks and months, you'll be astonished at how much improvement you can grab in your pursuit of the more challenging standards. If your goal is a complete fitness makeover, or to cultivate your potential to run fast for your chosen sport, be steadfast in putting in that little bit of focused work, like brushing and flossing your teeth, every day. Keep a training journal to record your progress, and keep an eye on your performance against the standards. This is the secret to being Ready to Run for a lifetime.

By investing 10 minutes a day over weeks and months, you'll be astonished at how much improvement you can grab.

CHAPTER 4
STANDARD #1: NEUTRAL FEET

Q: Are your feet habitually in a neutral position?

A neutral foot position simply means that when you're standing, walking, or running, your feet are straight. They aren't pigeon-toed in or splayed out like a duck's feet. They're straight.

NEUTRAL, STRAIGHT FEET. This is the position you want to use as much as you can throughout the day.

DUCK FEET. This position leads to an assortment of problems. Standing, walking, and running with this sort of mechanical collapse is a habit that will slowly eat you alive.

BIASED & UNBALANCED. This is an example of a lack of attention being paid to a good standing position. One foot is flared outward, the other neutral. Notice how the pelvic girdle tilts.

KEY MOTIVATION

By maintaining your feet in a neutral position while standing, walking, and running, you're setting the stage for efficient movement, defined as the way your body was engineered to move. And when you move your body in the way it was intended to move, you reduce the stresses that lead to injuries and worn-out joints.

BRIEFING

In essence, running is a series of jumps. With each jump, your foot makes contact with the ground; this is known as a foot strike. And in that instant, your body seeks stability. It has to be stable, or you'll fall.

The neutral position, in which your feet are straight and parallel to one another, is the most stable position for your feet. It's the way your musculoskeletal system was intended to land on the ground when you're running.

Let's take a look at what happens when you don't land with a neutral foot. Say your foot lands with an inward

recommended mobility exercises for neutral feet

Neutral feet start in your trunk, so really go after those tight hips:

- Couch Stretch (page 114)
- Adductor Smash (page 222)
- Anterior Hip Smash (page 223)
- Hamstring Floss (page 224)
- Double-Band Hip Distraction (page 232)
- Global Gut Smash (page 233)
- Glute Smash & Floss (page 235)
- Hip Capsule Rotation (page 237)

slant—pigeon-toed, in other words. Your system then needs to make specific compromises in your mechanics to generate the stability you need. Those compromises typically take a toll on your joints and the connective tissues of those joints. Run frequently enough with poor mechanics like these, and things will begin to wear out.

The neutral, stable foot position is a ready-for-action position that puts your body at its highest capacity for performance. It is at its most powerful when you also adopt a braced neutral spine, meaning that you are squeezing your glutes (often referred to as activating your hips) and your belly is tight. The tight belly pulls your ribcage down slightly so that your trunk is energized into a single unit. The final piece of a neutral spine is that your head is in alignment with your spine.

How do you make a habit of standing, walking, and running with neutral feet? Start by simply aligning your feet throughout the day, like tucking in your shirt or washing your hands. Run small spot checks throughout the day. Are your feet straight? If not, adjust them into a neutral position. Is your spine neutral? If not, take a breath and organize your spine, starting by squeezing your glutes and belly and then aligning your ribcage and head.

As I'll show you with the drills you'll use to work toward this standard, it starts with organizing your lower spine and clearing up any soft-tissue problems that might be working against you. But this standard is mostly about constant vigilance. Maintaining a neutral foot and spine position throughout the day cannot be an afterthought.

Adopting the neutral foot standard is simple, but it requires daily practice. It's the first step in assuming responsibility for the health of your feet—and breaking away from the idea that to be able to run throughout your life, all you need to do is sneak in a daily workout and outsource the injury problems to whatever your health insurance will cover. This is also the beginning of your freedom from the mistaken

Long periods of sitting that atrophy your joints and muscles; shoes that jack up your heels and weaken your heel cords; the rolled-shoulders and slumped-head position that so many people adopt: These are just a few of the debilitating practices that work together to weaken your feet and collapse your arches.

idea that a new pair of running shoes is an effective form of medical intervention.

Modern living is unkind when it comes to developing and maintaining neutral feet, with the myriad muscles, bones, and connective tissues empowered and activated into the steel springs that your arches were designed to be.

Long periods of sitting that atrophy your joints and muscles; shoes that jack up your heels and weaken your heel cords; the rolled-shoulders and slumped-head position that so many people adopt to read Facebook posts on their phones: These are just a few of the debilitating practices that work together to weaken your feet and collapse your arches, and that motivate runners to spend money on new shoes, orthotics, or medical care in the hopes that they will fix the problem.

Often, the money spent on trying to remedy the issue—the latest $150 running shoe combined with an over-the-counter arch support or an additional heel lift—may offer temporary relief. The runner can run again, or evade pain long enough to persevere through a goal marathon or ultramarathon. But a shoe designed to restrict natural foot motion only serves to deepen the problem. A dependency on running shoes, orthotics, ibuprofen, and heel-striking (see page 71) to maintain a weekly running mileage is why injury rates for runners remain at epidemic levels and why so many runners have been permanently sidelined to reading magazines while toiling away on an elliptical machine.

In other words, the high-tech running shoe intervention acts like a cast, rendering lifeless the incredible facilities of your feet. They erode, atrophy, and weaken. The steel springs that your feet were meant to be, with all the remarkable elasticity that is critical to running fast, running long, and enjoying a lifetime of running, rusts away.

Is the stability running shoe a solution?

How much is spent on running shoes in the United States? Three billion dollars a year. That's big money—a big investment in technology and a lot of computer modeling and fussing around with EVA foam, special cushioning, and stabilizing gadgets embedded into the midsole, all with an undertow of promises. As Christopher McDougall points out in his book *Born to Run,* the motion-control and stability technologies offered in today's running shoes can create more problems than they solve.

Here's a quick primer on how running shoes are typically categorized and marketed. There are three main divisions: cushioning shoes, stability shoes, and motion-control shoes. The template that has been in place since the 1980s is that you pick a shoe based on the amount of pronation you exhibit— how much your foot collapses inward on the foot strike. Certain running shoe stores and physical therapy clinics use some form of gait analysis and may watch you run or videotape you on a treadmill. If you are categorized as a mild pronator, you are advised to buy a cushioned shoe. If you're somewhere between being a mild pronator and being a severe pronator, you're matched with a stability shoe. If you're a real clunker of a pronator, they bring out the boat-like, super-stiff shoes that have been forebodingly engineered for "motion control."

(As I'll report in the next chapter, massive studies performed by the U.S. Army have shown that this model of matching runners with running shoes doesn't work at all.)

Overbuilt running shoes, costing small fortunes, tend to be the worst. The heel cushion the size of an ice cream sandwich? The patented plastic stability system baked into the EVA foam? This is more about the science of marketing than any valid science of injury prevention.

Wait a minute, you might be thinking. *You mean that all the talk we hear about the arms race that exists between running shoe companies in trademarked technologies—motion-control devices, stability features, rear-foot control design, foot bridges, and so on—there's no valid injury prevention research behind it?*

No, there isn't. There's no research to support the industry model that is marketed to you—that if you choose the right shoe for "your" foot with the right orthotics for "your" arch, run on the right surfaces, and change those shoes every 500 miles, you'll be healthier for it and avoid grinding away cartilage and shredding tendons.

The underlying marketing principle propelling this model boils down to this:

The motion of running is so dangerous that you always have to be on the right surface and in the right shoe.

This belief helps generate that $3 billion per year in running shoe sales. Yet the injury rate continues its march, to the tune of almost all runners getting injured at least once a year.

Are you okay with that?

The arch: A fundamental misunderstanding

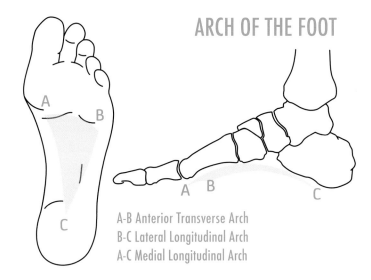

ARCH OF THE FOOT

A-B Anterior Transverse Arch
B-C Lateral Longitudinal Arch
A-C Medial Longitudinal Arch

Contrary to long-held beliefs, the arch of the foot is a non-weight-bearing surface. The idea that ligaments stretch out and the arch collapses buys into the misconception that the arch needs to be held up by something else. I am pro-orthotic in about .001 percent of patients who have them. If you are part of this .001 percent, it's because you are so destroyed that it hurts even to stand.

The arch of the foot is more than ligaments connecting bony structures. It is really a combination of arches: the medial longitudinal arch, lateral longitudinal arch, and anterior transverse arch—analogous to a suspension bridge or a leaf spring in a car.

Why would a $150 motion-control shoe be of any value? You don't seen any struts posts or structures supporting any of the arches that hold up bridges, right?

Exactly. The right choice is to revive the natural technologies you were born with. This begins with adhering to the Neutral Feet standard.

Achieving neutral feet

The first order of business is mindfulness. Right now, stand up and run a check on the position of your feet. They should be straight and parallel to one another, shoulder width apart, and directly under your hips. This is the neutral foot position. The objective of this standard is not simply to adopt this position while you run, but to adopt it *at all times*.

When your feet are in a neutral position and you supply your entire system with torque by squeezing your butt, which rotates your hips, you can run, jump, sprint, land, lift, and move with more power. You also turn on your arches. In this position, your feet are at their most stable, and you're prepared to move safely.

the truth about barefoot power, high heels, and flip-flops

Both flip-flops and high-heeled shoes create artificial stiffness in the ankle, and the wearer begins to walk as if she has stiff ankles, with her feet turned out. Walking through collapsed arches and around the big toe results in destroyed arches, undue torsion forces on the plantar fascia, oblique loading on the heel cords, impinged ankles, big bunions, and valgus knees. (Read more about the flip-flops problem on page 75.)

Look at cultures that go barefoot, and you see beautiful arches and strong feet. In cultures that habitually wear flip-flops, you see the nightmare described above. The Hawaiians even have a name for it: "island feet." Flip-flops are banned in our gym; we don't let our athletes wear them. We have solved countless cases of knee pain in our clinic simply by removing the flip-flop.

Your ankles and feet are hidden pools of physical reserve. Don't go wasting them. Want to see how ridiculous flip-flops really are? Run a quick 400 in them. I'll wait. Yeah, I know. You can't run at all. (Frankenstein slipper-shuffling isn't running.)

Mr. Miyagi was right: "Best defense, no be there."

Brace yourself

To light up the neutral foot position with power from your trunk, you need to make sure that the power switch is turned to the on position. To do so, perform the bracing sequence.

Why the bracing sequence? Spinal positions can be divided into three types:

OVEREXTENSION: A broken position with the pelvis tilted forward

FLEXION: A rounded-back posture

NEUTRAL: A balanced pelvis and the basis for a strong, protected midline

What you want to cultivate, both in your daily life and in your athletic training, is a neutral spine. This is an invaluable discipline for a runner, and, given the variety of movement patterns involved, even more so for a CrossFitter who runs or a football player who runs and also gets periodically slammed.

If you make a daily habit of maintaining neutral feet and a neutral spine (or "midline"), this foundational position will translate to your running. The benefits of midline stabilization go far beyond simply protecting you from lower back pain and injury. It also serves as the primary link in the flow of power through what is known as the posterior chain—the large, powerful muscles of the back, hips, hamstrings, and calves. When you run in a neutral position, the power flows, and you have the opportunity for greater activation and use of the large muscles of your hips and hamstrings.

When you're running in a broken position, either in overextension or in a rounded-back state of flexion, the link is broken. The posterior chain is effectively shut down, making you vulnerable to an assortment of injuries. All of a sudden, you're like the *Starship Enterprise* in Romulan territory, and you've turned off the shields.

The first step toward embracing the benefits of midline stabilization is to learn the bracing sequence. Periodically making sure that you are standing, walking, and running with neutral feet, as well as practicing a neutral spine, is what I call "building your training into your day." As you go about your life—work, family responsibilities, errands, chores—you can be training to be a better runner, a better athlete, or a better CrossFitter. You just need to make it a part of your ongoing routine. The more you practice it in the 23 hours a day that you're not running or working out, the more likely you are to do it during your workout.

Try the following sequence barefoot to get a sense of how it connects the trunk stability generated in your torso through the arches of your feet. Most of the time, sloppy foot positions are expressions of a sloppy spine position. A simple execution of the bracing sequence will draw you into good position.

Again, do the bracing sequence often throughout the day—so often that you don't even think about it anymore. Follow these steps:

1. Squeeze your butt the way a ballet dancer does, activating your glutes. This will set your pelvis in a neutral position.

2. To pull your ribcage down into a neutral position, breathe in through your diaphram, tighten your abs, and then slowly exhale. Imagine that your pelvis and your ribcage are two large bowls filled to the top with water. You want them both balanced so that neither spills a drop. Use your ab muscles to lock in the positions of your pelvis and ribcage. Squeezing your glutes provides the foundation for this position, and tightening your abs locks it all together.

3. Set your head in a neutral position, and then extend your arms out to the sides and pull your shoulders back into external rotation. With a balanced pelvis and ribcage, align your ears with your shoulders and hips. Your gaze is forward, and your hips, shoulders, and head are in a neutral position. This completes the picture. Now dial it all down to about 20 percent power. Maintaining a neutral position for your spine, shoulders, and head, take this out into the world with you by relaxing all the squeezing energy from a full effort to about a quarter effort. With practice, you can make this 20 percent engagement part of your normal ready state. (At his CrossFit Endurance seminar, Brian MacKenzie teaches athletes to run with 35 percent of the core turned on, with no negative effect on breathing.)

The benefits? Support for your spine that opens up the vast channel of power within your posterior chain that is waiting to be tapped. You become more durable and more efficient, and you prioritize the larger muscles over the smaller muscles, which equates to more endurance and stamina. While it's relatively easy to burn out your hip flexors (see Chapter 8), your glute muscles can just keep going and going and going.

do you walk like a duck?

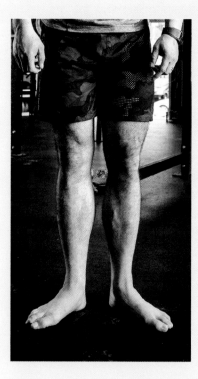

When your feet are turned out duck-style, stability bleeds away. With each step, your body has to work extra hard to compensate for the loss. The arch of your foot flattens out, your knee caves in, you lose power, and stresses on the soft tissues of your joints begin to pile up.

Keep your eyes open in the park or at a race and watch the duck-footed runners carefully. Watch what happens when their feet strike the ground. Observe the path of their ankles and knees. This is what you'll see: The feet are splayed outward. As the force of gravity goes to work on the body mass, the arches collapse, the ankles cave inward, and the knees follow the same path. This inward system collapse against the midline of the body is a deformity known as a valgus movement.

This oblique load, falling through a compromised skeletal system, exerts shearing forces through your joints and their soft tissues. Also, when your feet are turned out, your quad ligament gets pulled off axis and is no longer perpendicular to your kneecap—an essential point of alignment. Multiply these twisting forces by the number of steps you take in a 4-mile run, or a 10-mile run, or a marathon, or a year of running. Does it come as any surprise that runners cultivate medical problems like Achilles tendinopathy and patella tendinitis?

Runner to Runner

One of the compound exercises that is widely prescribed for runners is the back squat. This isn't a new phenomenon. In the 1994 book *Training Distance Runners,* by David Martin and Peter Coe, a great American cross-country runner of the time, eight-time national champion Pat Porter, is photographed doing barbell squats. Porter (who tragically was killed in a plane crash in 2012) was skinny looking, even for a 10,000-meter Olympian, which is saying something. The first time I saw him run in person, the word *spider* came to mind. Yet he was a ferocious and gutsy front-runner type who had become part of the lore of Alamosa, Colorado, where he lived and trained through the 1980s under the charismatic tutelage of Dr. Joe Vigil, the great exercise physiologist and coach who later became a star character in Christopher McDougall's bestseller *Born to Run.* At any rate, Porter is pictured in the classic running book deep into a barbell squat.

I first did squats with a loaded barbell in high school in my football days. I can tell you right now that my technique was probably not only bad, but dangerous. I recall purposefully caving in my knees because I felt like I could generate more power that way. Just as bad and possibly worse is that I never braced my lower spine before attempting a squat.

As the years went on, I occasionally revisited squatting for distance running, probably inspired by that picture of Pat Porter. I always seemed to be on the verge of some catastrophic injury, so eventually I let them go.

In working with Kelly Starrett and Brian MacKenzie on the overhaul of my running life, two of the first things I learned were how to squat safely and how to brace my spine and keep it braced—not just for squats, but also for standing, sitting, walking, and running.

It was odd at first, particularly working to maintain a braced spine while running. The breathing took some time to figure out, and, at first, anyway, holding the brace seemed to take considerable energy.

But there's no going back after you've practiced it awhile. If I let those muscles go, I can feel the vulnerabilities of the unbraced spine creeping back in. I can also feel the power connection between my core and my legs slip away.

Another valuable upshot of adopting a braced neutral spine is this: When you do perform squats using good technique (which you'll learn in Chapter 7), it makes a huge difference in protecting your spine. The heavier the weight, the more you'll notice. Despite all my years of running plenty of miles with weak mechanics that brought with them a history of lower back problems, I can squat with loads well over my body weight without the slightest sketchy sensation. And my back has never felt healthier and stronger.

The bracing sequence is why.

—T.J. Murphy

CHAPTER 5
STANDARD #2: FLAT SHOES

Q: **Do you wear flat shoes?**

This standard is as uncomplicated as it is robustly effective: When you wear shoes, wear the flat kind. If you're walking the red carpet on Oscar night, fine, go ahead and wear a shoe with a heel. Once in a while is okay. But most of the time, you should wear shoes that are flat and won't throw your biological movement hardware into disarray. When you have to wear shoes, whether it's running shoes, work shoes, or combat boots, buy the flat kind, also known as having "zero drop"— meaning that the heel is not raised above the forefoot. What you want to avoid, or wean yourself away from, are shoes with the heels raised higher off the ground than the forefeet.

KEY MOTIVATION

It may seem like a minor deviation that your running shoes (for instance) have half an inch more cushion under the heel than the forefoot, but this seemingly minor tweak is like messing with the springs on a race car. It screws up the whole system, and at some point, the wheels are going to burn off.

Consider the null hypothesis in regard to shoes, feet, and running. The null hypothesis refers to who in a debate about medical treatment shoulders the burden of proof. It takes into account what the default position or situation is. In regard to running, the default position for your feet is to be barefoot. So those who insist that a running shoe should have an elevated heel and be loaded with stability technology to restrict motion, and maybe an orthotic, too, have to prove that being barefoot is a broken state that requires fixing.

You're going to have to wear shoes because you work in an office or you walk or run on a sidewalk, which is provably dangerous if you don't have thick calluses on your feet. You want a shoe that protects your foot from rocks and broken glass and/or allows you not to get written up by HR, yet allows your foot to function as naturally as possible.

BRIEFING

When you run, do you land on your heels? If you do, then it's fair to assume that you're wearing a running shoe that has a big, fat chunk of cushion under the heel. This shoe effectively jacks your heel up higher off the ground than your forefoot.

Running shoe ads have long been deployed to show off how potent heel-cushion technology is (be it air, gel, space-age rubber, or some honeycomb thing), and the photo of the runner in the ad is taken right at the point of the heel's impact with the ground. There's a smile on the euphoric and skinny runner's face, even though her leg is snapped into full extension out in front of her body, jamming her calcaneus

recommended mobility exercises for flat shoes

Don't just put on a pair of minimalist shoes. Help bring your feet and arches back to life with these exercises:

- Plantar Mobilizations (page 217)
- Toe Grip (page 220)
- Toe Re-animator (page 221)
- Calf Smash (page 205)

into the concrete, buffered by the pillow of cushion injected into the compression-molded midsole. What would be great is to have a physicist take a scientific calculator to the image and extrapolate how much in the way of braking forces are shock-waving their way through the runner's skeleton and transmitting various shearing forces to the soft tissues within her joints, then take that data and multiply it by the number of steps taken in a mile and the number of miles run in a week, month, or year, and graph that data against the number and severity of injuries incurred by this runner.

So there's controversy—some say that the runner in this picture is heel-striking. And what of it? It's the natural way she runs, isn't it?

It isn't. In fact, I promise that if you had her take off the shoes and run 100 meters down a sidewalk, the heel-striking would vaporize instantly. She wouldn't be landing on her heel or mid-foot; she would be landing on her forefoot.

You were born to run, but you weren't born to heel-strike when you run. Is there any gray area here? No, there isn't. Small children don't heel-strike. Unfortunately, they are absorbed by a dysfunctional system that we have long been warned about (see the sidebar "Shoes for Children" on page 74).

If you're heel-striking, you have to stop. It's eating you alive.

If you're heel-striking when you run, you have to stop. It's eating you alive.

From what I've observed, you don't start seeing kids heel-strike until about the first grade. Then it starts kicking in—hours spent sitting at desks and wearing shoes with heels, setting them on a path where the feet weaken, the arches collapse, and the heel cords shorten, robbing them of the natural power of their feet. Want to do your children a big favor? Put them in flat shoes early on and keep them there.

I'm not saying to wear shoes all the time. In fact, I want you and your family to embrace Barefoot Saturday. One day a week, make a concerted effort to be barefoot as much as

Make a concerted effort to be barefoot as much as possible in order to strengthen and mobilize your feet.

possible. As long as you're walking around in places where you know there's no glass or debris that might harm your feet, go barefoot. When you're walking around the house or backyard is another good chance to safely be barefoot and sneak in a session of secret training—a nice dose of strengthening and mobilizing your feet.

Nick Campitelli is a runner and podiatrist in Akron, Ohio, and publishes Dr. Nick's Running Blog. When Dr. Nick was going through podiatry school, he couldn't help but look at it through the lens of a distance runner, since injured runners rely on podiatrists to help keep them healthy and logging miles on the road. Certain things he learned troubled him. For one, he couldn't find a single thread of research that supported building up the heel cushion in a running shoe over and above the forefoot—a running shoe industry transition that started in the 1970s.

Back in the 1960s, everyone was running in flat shoes—Keds, Converse, Onitsuka (aka Asics) Tigers. Then air cushions and the like began to get stuffed under the heel, but for no clear and definitive reason that Campitelli could sort out. His best guess was that someone had some heel pain and raised the heel to limit the pain, and then someone else thought, "Why don't we do this with an entire line of running shoes?" Whatever the reason, the change appears to have been driven by the industry and by marketing, Campitelli says. The upshot of the change was this: As running boomed, more and more heel-striking was enabled until heel-striking became standard.

But that doesn't mean it's right. Dr. Nick is unique in the podiatry world because when runners come to see him with an injury, his solution never involves an orthotic. Rather, he targets the abductor hallucis muscle, a muscle found on the medial side of the foot that has the unique and powerful job of abducting the big toe. (Refer to the illustration on page 78.) Dr. Nick's focus in helping a runner reconstitute his or her feet is slowly, patiently transitioning the runner from (for example) a big, honking motion-control shoe implanted with a wickedly stiff orthotic into a minimalistic shoe that is flat and flexible and lets the foot be a foot.

In the before-and-after photos taken of one of Dr. Nick's patients, you can see the result of his work. The photo on the left was taken when a 34-year-old woman runner came to see him for help. She had motion-control shoes and orthotics that weren't doing anything to prevent knee and back pain. Notice how her heels are leaning inward, on the verge of collapse? Both her heels and her knees were valgus. The motion-control-shoe-and-orthotic setup was supposed to realign her heels and the rest of her skeleton with them. How did that work out for her?

It took two years, but after slowly introducing a zero-drop shoe to his patient, Dr. Nick let nature take its course. As you can see in the photo on the right, the runner's calcaneus has been resurrected and is now practically vertical, restoring what was previously a collapsed arch. There was no use of "corrective" orthotics or stiff-shanked shoes. As Campitelli says, it's the simple product of a foot being allowed to be a foot.

"This is not the direct result of simply wearing a minimalist shoe," Campitelli says. "This is the result of what happens when you stress the foot and let it work the way it was intended to and become stronger."

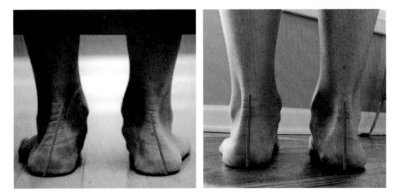

Dr. Campitelli's patient before and after. In 2012, she was a complete shipwreck. But after patient exposure to flat shoes and strengthening work, her arches and alignment were restored to original manufacturer's condition in 2014.

shoes for children

[8] Lynn T. Staheli, "Shoes for Children: A Review," *Pediatrics* 88, no. 2 (1991): 371-75.

Barefoot Saturday—spending one day a week being barefoot as much as possible—is good both for you and for your kids. In 1991, Dr. Lynn T. Staheli of the department of orthopedics at the Children's Hospital and Medical Center in Seattle published a review of shoes for children in *Pediatrics,* the journal of the American Academy of Pediatrics.[8] "Some physicians believe that shoes are simply part of the child's clothing, while others believe that shoes are important therapeutic tools capable of correcting deformity and preventing significant disability later in life," she writes, introducing an approach that "focuses on how the foot fares without shoes."

Dr. Staheli summarizes the findings, which she describes as being "based on objective data rather than impressions or tradition," as follows:

1. Optimum foot development occurs in the barefoot environment.
2. The primary role of shoes is to protect the foot from injury and infection.
3. Stiff and compressive footwear may cause deformity, weakness, and loss of mobility.
4. The term "corrective shoes" is a misnomer.
5. Shock absorption, load distribution, and elevation are valid indications for shoe modifications.
6. Shoe selection for children should be based on the barefoot model.
7. Physicians should avoid and discourage the commercialization and "media"-ization of footwear. Merchandising of the "corrective shoe" is harmful to the child, expensive for the family, and a discredit to the medical profession.

flip-flops? just say no

While barefoot, I want you to take a moment to appreciate one of the most vivid illustrations of how your body is a system of systems and why one of the best things you can do for these elaborate, highly evolved systems is to not screw them up.

Standing, look down at your right foot. Now watch and feel what happens when you slowly lift your toes. The arch turns on, doesn't it? Lifting the toes, especially the big toe, winds up the plantar fascia. In the same way you use a windlass mechanism to crank up a bucket of water from a deep well, your foot is a kind of biological winch, where the plantar fascia is the cable and the big toe is the crank. The windlass effect is how one went about hoisting rocks hundreds of feet into the air in the church construction business back in the fourteenth century. In your feet, the plantar fascia's windlass mechanics provide for an assortment of critical functions, according to Kevin Kirby, a professor of applied biomechanics, including arch support, reducing shearing forces on the ligaments and compression forces being fed into the joints, and absorbing elastic strain during the acts of running and jumping.[9]

So what's a great way to screw up your foot machines? Flip-flops. When you walk from point A to B, you have to clench your big toe to keep the thing from slipping off. And when you clench the big toe, the windlass system in your foot grinds to a halt, and your plantar fascia pays the price. The tissues of the arch get gummed up and shortened, messing with all the properties the plantar fascia is designed to deliver. The kink gets distributed through multiple systems, like a shortened heel cord to entrapping the sciatic nerve, which corresponds to Achilles pathologies and neurodynamic aches and pains. All because of flip-flops.

Sure, wear a pair of flip-flops in the shower room if you're wary of fungus. But if you want to be an athlete with full-on performance capacities, avoid them. They are the plague.

[9] Kevin Kirby, "Functions of the plantar fascia," www.podiatry-arena.com/podiatry-forum/showthread.php?t=1464 (January 2, 2006).

DROPPING DOWN TO ZERO

So you've been wearing heeled shoes all your life, you run in shoes with a 12mm drop, you lack dorsiflexion, and you suffer the consequences of having a valgus calcaneus and valgus knee.

There is no overnight fix.

You have to pony up and understand that making this change is going to take time. Don't be that guy who runs 60 miles a week and chucks his $150 motion-control shoes with a 12mm drop for a pair of zero-drop Vibrams and doesn't want a single hiccup in the logbook. Your chances of being injured by too much stress, too quickly, are high. Maybe certain.

But know this: Your feet have the power to change.

Here's the protocol that Dr. Nick Campitelli recommends:

- **Choose a pair of minimalist shoes that you like.** The shoe should allow you to be as close to barefoot as you're comfortable with. Look for zero drop and zero arch support.
- **Plan on a minimum of six to eight weeks to transition into your new shoes.** Longer is fine. Shorter is not. In the grand scheme of things, two months is not a big deal when it comes to your running life.
- **Use the 10 percent rule.** If you're heading out for a 3-mile run, run one-third of a mile (10 percent of your total distance) at the beginning of your run in your new minimalist shoes. Then change into whatever your regular shoe setup has been, orthotics and all. Why wear the minimalist shoe at the *beginning* of your run? Because your feet are fresh.
- **Each week, increase the amount of time you spend running in your new minimalist shoes by 10 percent.** Exercise caution throughout the process—listen to your feet. Add a week with no change here and there if you need to.

A WORD ON WORK SHOES

Here's a field trip assignment for you. Visit the mall at lunchtime on a weekday and hover around the men's shoe stores. Be on the lookout for the iconic businessman making a stop to bolster his wardrobe. Does he fit the following description?

He wears a tailored dark suit and a pair of dress shoes. The shoes have the stylish configuration of vamp, quarter, and heel cap, and beneath the heel cap is a firm, blocky heel, raising the rear of his foot significantly above the plane of his forefoot. Watch the businessman stride around confidently—striking out with long steps, eating up territory, forcefully heel-striking out in front of his body. You've seen this before, and there's a form of social power to the imagery. Notice how this style of movement is enabled by the construction of the shoe.

Now that you've seen it, do the exact opposite and transition toward flat shoes—not just for running and kicking around, but also for wearing to the office or job site. In progressing your foot toward full work capacity, you want to effectively cancel out any time spent in a shoe that shortens your tendons and kills off the range of motion that your foot was designed to wield.

want to control excessive pronation? train your abductor hallucis muscles

[10] Yue Shuen Wong, "Influence of the Abductor Hallucis Muscle on the Medial Arch of the Foot: A Kinematic and Anatomical Cadaver Study," *Foot & Ankle International* 28, no. 5 (2007): 617-20.

[11] P. Fiolkowski, D. Brunt, M. Bishop, R. Woo, and M. Horodyski, "Intrinsic Pedal Musculature Support of the Medial Longitudinal Arch: An Electromyography Study," *Journal of Foot and Ankle Surgery* 42, no. 6 (2003): 327-33.

The abductor hallucis muscle has the job of abducting the big toe. When it is strong and supple, this key postural muscle brings your foot to life. By simply wearing flat shoes (and spending as much time as you can barefoot), you will give your abductor hallucis muscles the workout they need and deserve.

When it comes to running injuries, excessive pronation (inward rolling of the foot) is often considered the guilty culprit. For years, the common answer has been to steer the injured runner into a stability or motion-control shoe, along with an over-the-counter arch support or a custom-made orthotic, to the tune of $100 or more. Is your foot overpronating? Then wear a stiff shoe that acts like a brace on your foot, conventional wisdom says.

Here's a different idea, one that's ridiculously cheaper: Train your abductor hallucis muscles. Essentially, the abductor hallucis originates from the heel bone and travels along the inside of the foot, inserting at the base of your big toe. The work that the abductor hallucis does in support of your arch is profound: It's involved in the flexion and abduction of your big toe, the rotation of your tibia, and the inversion of your heel (the calcaneus).[10] Studies using electromyography have demonstrated that this muscle plays a critical role in controlling pronation.[11]

But this happens only when your foot isn't in a state of physical erosion. So, rather than further weaken your foot with a shoe-brace contraption, commit to Barefoot Saturday, wear flat shoes when you must wear shoes, and put in consistent mobility work to wake up and strengthen your toes.

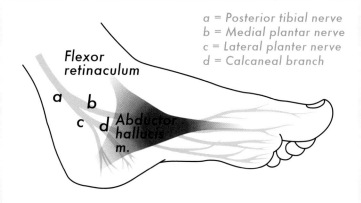

Flexor retinaculum

a = Posterior tibial nerve
b = Medial plantar nerve
c = Lateral planter nerve
d = Calcaneal branch

a   b
c d   *Abductor hallucis m.*

Runner to Runner

Over the past 25 years of running, I have suffered a multitude of injuries around my Achilles tendon area. My response was to ice it two or three times for a couple of days and then start stretching out the ankle. At whatever point I resumed running (if I took any break at all), I inserted pads into the heels of my running shoes. The shoe, it should be mentioned, often had a significantly built-up heel over the height of the forefoot. I never even thought to address whatever sort of issue was the cause of the injury.

Once when I was averaging 80 to 90 miles of running per week, my left Achilles flared in a painfully tender way. Training slammed to a halt. My coach said, "One thing about high-mileage running: If you have any mechanical problems, it will bring them to the surface." A good analysis, but unhelpful. I was desperate to resume my running program full bore. Perhaps a better decision would have been to make ferreting out the mechanical issue my top priority. Such a choice might have prevented the considerable bunion I have on my left heel.

Better late than never, I now address mechanical issues with running drills. I also mobilize with the exercises outlined in Part 3 of this book, sliding surface work with a soft ball, and range of motion work. The final part of the picture for me is wearing flat shoes. Given that I sought out fat, cushioned heels in training shoes and wore running shoes in my daily life as well, the transition was a delicate one. At first I would notice within 20 minutes a low-grade pain from the stress. More was being asked of my heel cords. It took a couple of months of progressive exposure until I had adjusted to wearing flat shoes all the time. The interesting thing to report is that putting on a pair of shoes that has a high drop from heel to toe is weirdly uncomfortable for me now. I hate it. Flat shoes actually feel better.

—TJM

CHAPTER 6
STANDARD #3: A SUPPLE THORACIC SPINE

Q: **Do you have a pliant, properly organized thoracic spine?**

The 12 thoracic vertebrae of your middle back are not to be forgotten. While runners tend to think a lot about the muscles and joints from the lower back down through the feet, the thoracic spine, or T-spine, is crucial when it comes to being able to sustain a neutral position in your long-distance running. If you haven't given much thought to taking care of your middle back (when you run, sit, walk, talk, type, text, breathe, and so on), then it's time to start changing that today.

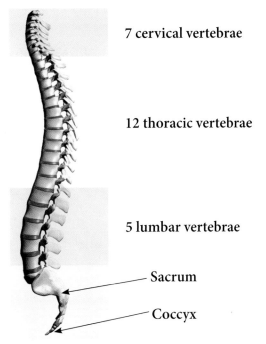

7 cervical vertebrae

12 thoracic vertebrae

5 lumbar vertebrae

— Sacrum

— Coccyx

KEY MOTIVATION

While we hear a lot about how important "the core" is to running—the core typically being defined as the bottom of the ribcage to mid-thigh or so, depending on who you're listening to—be aware that if your T-spine is tight and out of whack, then all the power that you'd like to have flowing from your hard-earned six-pack and taut glute muscles is going to get squeezed off. A tight thoracic spine gums up your posterior chain, and you can't get your shoulders and head into a good, aligned position, which transmits strain into your neck and lower back. It can also mess with your hip function, so stresses will seep and creep their way into the usual suspects: knees, ankles, and feet. And the longer you go in a run, the more your form disintegrates, and the uglier it gets.

recommended mobility exercises for a supple thoracic spine

Start wailing on your T-spine and shoulders with these gems:

- T-Spine Global Smash (page 244)
- T-Spine Double-Ball Strip (page 245)
- Anterior Shoulder (page 246)

BRIEFING

Every weekday morning in San Francisco, herds of high-tech workers line up at street corners, waiting for the charter bus to swing by and load them up for their daily trip to Silicon Valley. They take their seats on the bus and jack into the Wi-Fi with their laptops, but you see them getting their start while waiting for the bus, many of them hunched up, shoulder rolled, heads hanging out over the cliff, at one with their iPhones, either reading or texting. They will spend the better part of the day honing this ungodly position.

They are not alone, of course. The modern runner is often the modern desk athlete. Unless you're vigilant about your positions, that's a big problem. Of these two images, which sounds like it's doing more damage to the body?

The modern runner is often the modern desk athlete. Unless you're vigilant about your positions, that's a big problem.

- **A day laborer in India transporting bricks to a construction site in a basket perched on top of her head.**
- **A computer programmer hunched over his laptop with a 7-ounce baseball cap on his head. For the sake of connection, let's say he's one of the tech workers waiting for the Google bus on the corner of 18th and Dolores in San Francisco's Mission District. He starts his day with his head hanging over his phone, and then he climbs into a window seat on the bus and spends the rest of the day caving his head and shoulders over a computer.**

Let me put it this way: In this comparison, the woman in her sari carrying bricks is showing off the power of midline stabilization. The programmer, on the other hand, is committing himself to a slow and grisly death.

Say that programmer is training for a half-marathon. If he's spending six, eight, or more hours a day slouched over a screen of some kind, mastering what might be called the Pooping Dog position, do you think it might translate through osmosis to how he runs?

One of the things that's definitely going to happen is that, after he practices it for 40, 50, or more hours a week, this broken position is going to feel very normal to him.

And this is what you're going to see if you spend some time watching the hundreds of people run by in a road race: rounded upper backs—which is an expression of a tight thoracic spine—with heads jutting out in front of spines.

The consequences of a tight thoracic spine

What are the consequences of a tight thoracic spine and a broken upper body, neck, and head position? Because the human body is a system of systems, the dysfunction is broadcast up and down the kinetic chain and manifests itself in problems throughout the body:

- **Neck pain.** When you see that head jutting out in front of the spine, consider that the head weighs about 12 pounds on its own and that every inch it juts forward effectively adds another 10 pounds of weight to the problem.
- **Shoulder mobility problems.** When your shoulder joints are in a neutral, externally rotated position, you get the benefit of stored-up energy from rotational torque. With your shoulders rolled forward, you give up all this torque. Your soft tissues have a lot more stress put on them, and they have to stabilize the shoulder joints. As the woman who carries a basket full of bricks on her head knows intuitively, an organized skeleton with the shoulders properly set in a neutral position channels the power of structural support to stabilize the situation, whereas a poor position grinds away at the soft tissues. Even though the deskbound distance runner isn't carrying a load on top of his head, if his posture is broken and midline stabilization

is lost, his shoulders are going to pay a price. Why would a runner have trouble getting his arms over his head? The fact is that he shouldn't.

- **Lower back pain.** A tight, hunched thoracic spine shuts down the flow of power within the body's systems. In running, this translates to more stress being dumped on the lower back, or lumbar section of the spine.

- **Knee pain.** Without a neutral spine, stress on the knees increases. Now we're in the territory of some of the ailments that runners are more familiar with: piriformis pain (aka deep butt pain) and any number of knee ailments that result from poor hip function.

- **Other hotspots.** Again, the body is a system of systems. In my model, your trunk is the chassis of your Formula 1 running machine. The two primary engines for power are the hips and shoulders. A tight thoracic spine gums up stability and the flow of power. This invites any number of kinks into the complex operation of stabilizing the body while running, including how your foot strikes the ground. The result is pain. Feeling pain is a clear sign that you're doing something wrong.

- **Loss of power.** This discussion isn't just about pain. It's also about power. Consider again that your trunk is the chassis, and you have an engine in your hips and an engine in your shoulders. If you run with your shoulders hunched forward and your head jutting out over your faulty upper back position, you are bleeding away power.

A tight, hunched thoracic spine shuts down the flow of power within the body's systems.

If you have neck pain, or your shoulders roll forward because they are lacking external rotation, or you have a problem downstream because there's so much stress and weirdness going on in your lower back and hips, then pay close attention to this standard. A supple, organized thoracic spine is the place to start.

Achieving a supple thoracic spine

To get into good position, follow these steps:

Standing with a neutral spine, squeeze your shoulder blades together to externally rotate your shoulders so that the joints are set properly.

Move your arms into a relaxed, 90-degree position, retaining neutral midline stability and correct shoulder position.

THE DREADED ROLLED-SHOULDERS FAULT. This is what you don't want to look like. Notice that my shoulders are inwardly rotated right out of the joint sockets. This is no way to run 10 miles.

In addition to practicing the bracing sequence (see page 65) throughout the day, use the mobilizations that target the upper back (found on pages 244–245) to breathe some air into your thoracic spine.

Runner to Runner

Upper body running form used to be an oxymoron for me. The stretching routine that I performed over the years didn't include a single move that attended to anything above my lower back. One of the reasons I never thought about it was probably because I occasionally trained with a runner who had a 2:20 marathon to his credit, much faster than my PR. He hunched his shoulders in such a way when he ran that his posture reminded me of Mr. Burns from *The Simpsons*. I've known many good runners over the years who run with their shoulders rolled over and inward and their backs hunched. It didn't seem to slow them down, either, so who cares? As it turns out, I care.

Another ailment that I picked up over the years was a pain in my neck, like having a long, thin needle plunged into my upper spine. I would feel it when I ran or walked for a long time. Placing a lacrosse ball on the tissue along my thoracic spine made a difference immediately. In addition to pain management, I've learned (the hard way) that having a properly organized upper spine and shoulders takes less energy. In other words, if the skeleton is allowed to do its job, less energy needs to be expended by the muscles doing the work of keeping things stable and lifted.

—TJM

CHAPTER 7
STANDARD #4: AN EFFICIENT SQUATTING TECHNIQUE

Q: **Can you squat correctly?**

This standard is about good hip function and good ankle function. Being able to perform a deep squat using good movement patterns, with proper hip function—and having a visceral understanding of what these patterns are—is foundational in being Ready to Run. Achieving this standard also means being able to perform a sequence of good squats under a small dose of metabolic load.

There are two tests involved with this standard:

- **Can you perform a squat with good technique, using the patterns your body is designed to squat with?**
- **Can you maintain a minimum of 10 good, clean air squats within the Tabata interval protocol; meaning, can you maintain a pace of 10 good air squats in 8 consecutive periods of 20 seconds, with 10 seconds of rest after each period?**

KEY MOTIVATION

Being able to squat well is the foundation of good movement patterns that enable you to access power from your posterior chain and protect you from injury. Meeting this standard will translate to proper hip function and an understanding of what good mechanics feel like.

recommended mobility exercises for efficient squatting

The best way to improve your squat is, believe it or not, to do a lot of squats and spend time in a deep squatting position. Also bias these mobilizations:

- Couch Stretch (page 114)
- Banded Ankle Mob (page 206)
- Posterior Chain Banded Floss (page 238)
- Low-Back Ball Smash (page 242)
- 10-Minute Squat Test (www.mobilitywod.com/2010/08/episode-01-the-first-of-many-beat-downs/)

BRIEFING

You've probably heard that most runners have "weak hips." Another description is that the glutes "aren't firing" or are "shut down" or "imbalanced." Here's a performance motivator for you: Analyzing, fixing, and developing your squatting ability will reward you with the ability to activate your all-powerful glutes when you run and open up a clean flow of hip drive into your running. Have you experienced that run where you have a lot of pop off the ground and feel like you're flying? That's hip drive.

Also: Do you want to expose any dysfunction in your mechanics that may be grinding you up with chronic injury? There's no more direct and effective way to illuminate your movement problems than squatting. And that's not all. As famed running coach and author Dr. Jack Daniels will tell you, the threat of running injury increases when you fatigue in a run or race and your mechanics go to hell.

Would some insight into how you hold up a good pattern be of any use to you? Knowledge is power, so glean even more information by adding a dose of endurance stress to your squat testing. This helps you get your mind around what's mangled or missing in the movement patterns that are fundamental to your running performance and your running health. Good movement patterns should be in place at the beginning of a run and should look the same at the finish. As a bonus, knowing how to squat well is going to make you a better, more functional person—you won't have to wave off your neighbor when she asks if you can help move a sofa bed because you're afraid that you'll get hurt. You'll be better able to climb and descend stairs like a healthy person as opposed to a broken runner who navigates steps like land mines.

Some years ago, a top American middle-distance runner had qualified to run the 1,500 meters in the World Championships. The times he was producing in the summer racing season indicated that he had a chance to medal. But he never made the trip to Worlds. Why? Because one day he was mowing the lawn and threw his back out.

This is what I'm talking about. Being a runner shouldn't mean that you can't lift a box or push a baby stroller without the threat of a season-ending injury. Developing and mastering your squat will give both your running and your life a boost.

The following two squat tests will serve you well as a diagnostic tool and will help guide you with your ongoing mobility work.

Being a runner shouldn't mean that you can't lift a box or push a baby stroller without the threat of a season-ending injury. Developing and mastering your squat will give both your running and your life a boost.

Test #1: A good, basic air squat

To check your squatting mechanics, set up your phone or a camera to shoot video, or have a friend give you some real-time feedback. Your task is to do a squat with your hips dropping below your knees and then return to the starting position. You must achieve the following technique specifics:

1. **Stand with your feet just outside your shoulders—the classic power stance in athletics.** Imagine that you're going to do a standing long jump, or you're getting into position to chase after a tennis serve from Venus Williams. Position your feet straight or slightly open. Slightly open is okay—but just slightly. A duck-footed stance, with your toes pointing too far outward, is a fault. Pigeon-toed inward is also a fault.

2. **Activate your butt and posterior chain.** With your feet straight, turn on the muscles of your posterior chain—from your arches to your hamstrings, hips, and muscles supporting your trunk—by pretending that you are screwing two dinner plates into the ground

with your feet. Your left foot exerts rotational energy in a counterclockwise direction, and your right foot in a clockwise direction. Extend your arms forward as a measure of counterbalance before you descend into the squat.

3. **Drive your knees outward.** Cue yourself to keep your heels on the ground and drive your knees outward to prevent any debilitating inward (valgus) knee movement.

4. **Drop your hips below the plane of your knees without extending your knees over your feet.** Notice the depth of my squat. Your air squat needs to be deep enough that the hip crease at the front of your leg drops below the plane of your knees. (continued on next spread)

5. **Keep your knees from extending over your feet.** Notice from the side how my knees don't break the vertical line that could be drawn upward from my toes. Leaching your knees out over your feet is a big fault to look out for. If you keep your shins vertical, you can unload stress from your knees and use your hips and hamstrings to do the work for the squat. Vertical shins enable you to take advantage of all that safe power and stability that the posterior chain can provide.

What you don't want to see are your knees driving out over and in front of your feet, with your shins breaking the vertical line. With that break comes shear and stress-wreaking havoc on your knees. If you see that you're making this fault, redo the squat with vertical shins, focus on loading your hips and hamstrings, and notice how little toll a deep squat takes on your knees. If you're doing it right, they will breeze through it.

Also take note of the flat back. Before beginning and throughout the execution of the squat, your glute and ab muscles should be active so that they can maintain a strong, neutral spine and a flat back. You should have a tightened midline, in other words. If you let these muscles go soft, the power flow of the posterior chain goes dead, and your squat will be "broken." Keep a good, flat back throughout the squat to pass this part of the test.

6. **Hang out in the squat position.** How do you develop mobility for a better squat? The same mobility that will reward you with better hip function for your running? By spending time in the squat position. I encourage athletes to collect 10 or more minutes a day in the squat position.

7. **Use a support.** If you're coming into this standard with weak, tight hips, shorted heel cords, and other mobility and strength restrictions, use a pole as a support to collect minutes in a deep squat position.

FAULT: valgus knees. A common fault for runners performing the air squat test is that their knees collapse inward into a valgus position, as shown above. The valgus position is a fault in which (especially under the load of a weighted barbell) you can practically see smoke coming out of the knees as the soft tissues burn. Watch your knees carefully. Just as they should not extend out in front of your feet, they should not collapse inward. Keep an eye on the arches of your feet as well— they should stay turned on as opposed to collapsing inward.

FAULT: duck feet. Duck feet are what typically lead to the valgus knee fault. In addition to driving your knees outward throughout the squat, be sure you use neutral feet as a preventative measure.

Test #2: The ability to do a lot of good squats when fatigued

You may have the ability to meet this standard easily right out of the gate, but I encourage you to check in with it frequently. It will help you keep an eye on things throughout the year and through the various fluctuations that might impact your training. Like if you ramp things up for a marathon. Or work goes off the rails. This is like a smog test. It will also give you a quick, no-impact workout, for whatever that's worth.

I started using the Tabata squat test as a marker for rehab with patients recovering from ACL surgery. In a compressed period, it reveals a lot about motor control patterns and range of motion in the ankle and hip. You definitely want to shoot video to see how you move under the duress of metabolic load. It makes the invisible visible.

Having or developing the capacity to do a good squat is a great start in meeting this standard. Not only do I want you to be able to do one correctly, but I want to encourage you to understand all the working parts of a good squat and what they feel like. Why? Because this knowledge will translate to how you monitor your running form.

My Tabata squat test for this standard is based on the Tabata interval protocol, following a series of 8 short, 20-second intervals and even shorter 10-second rests. Within each minute of a 4-minute period, you will perform two 20-second bouts of work, each followed by a 10-second breather.

This is a killer tool for exposing weaknesses in a safe environment. Tabata squats quickly introduce fatigue into the picture, but no one is going to get injured. Range of motion problems will surface, and by the end you'll see if you're favoring one side or the other.

This is also a killer tool for netting a universal feel for how to load your hips and hamstrings.

To achieve the squatting standard, you must do the following after a thorough warm-up: Perform a minimum of 10 quality air squats in every 20-second interval in a 4-minute workout. If you can do more than 10, that's great, but to achieve this standard, your count of good squats in each work interval should never drop below 10.

It looks like this:

Understanding the working parts of a good squat and what they feel like will translate to how you monitor your running form.

1. Do a thorough warm-up. This is considered a high-intensity workout, so warm up accordingly with air squats, jumping rope, burpees, push-ups, and mobility exercises. You should be hot and sweaty when you start the Tabata test.
2. Set up a video camera (or a friend or training partner) and a clock or timer. The work intervals and rest intervals come fast and furious, so be sure that you know when to squat and when to rest.
3. Keep your feet straight throughout the session. Be on the lookout for your feet wanting to turn outward. If they do, those squats don't count.
4. Begin the first 20-second work interval. Fire off good squats and start counting them. Perform as many quality squats as you can in 20 seconds.
5. Rest for 10 seconds. One of the things you'll figure out fast is that 10 seconds goes by quickly. Grab some air and be ready to execute another round of good squats.
6. Repeat this pattern for 4 minutes, counting the number of squats you do in each interval. If you break any of the rules of proper technique—like allowing your knees to cave inward or tracking your knees out over and beyond your feet—that rep doesn't count. Only good reps count.

If you can do at least 10 passable squats in each interval, you have achieved this standard. Work toward more! Go for 15 or more squats per interval and bake a good squat pattern into your body.

Runner to Runner

The strength programs I recall seeing in the 1980s and '90s usually recommended the following moves: knee extensions, hamstring curls, calf raises, and quarter squats on the leg press. There was a terrific aversion to the idea of a deep squat. As Kelly points out in a number of his range of motion recommendations, he does not advocate any hypermobile positions. *Normal* is what he's asking for. The same applies to the squat. If you can squat only a quarter of the way down, you're missing out on a huge swath of range that is key to simply being healthy.

From what I've learned in recent years, coaches may have settled on the quarter-range squat as being the safe squat simply because if you do the squat wrong—with your knees extending out over your feet and/or caving inward—then all the stress lands in the wrong spot: your knees. If you load your hips and hamstrings by lowering into a squat properly, you can feel the difference: There is practically zero stress on your knees. The power is being generated by the large muscles of your hips. These muscles are so large that they seem virtually inexhaustible. I've now performed workouts that include 300 squats, each requiring that I lower my hips beneath the plane of my knees. The major stress is on my lungs—you can bang these reps out by the dozen, and what slows you down is not the breakdown of muscle, but the amount of blood and oxygen required to feed them. I do squats every week now in one form or another, and as ironic as it might seem to coaches who say that runners shouldn't squat because it's too dangerous, I do them for the opposite reason: If I go a couple of weeks without squat work, my posture gets sloppy and my hip function suffers. I need the squats to prevent the kinds of injury pain that used to bite me all the time.

—TJM

CHAPTER 8
STANDARD #5: HIP FLEXION

Q: Can you stand on your left leg and express normal range of hip flexion with your right hip for 30 seconds, then repeat with your right leg and left hip?

[12] Paul E. Niemuth, Robert J. Johnson, Marcella Myers, and Thomas J. Thieman, "Hip Muscle Weakness and Overuse Injuries in Recreational Runners," *Clinical Journal of Sport Medicine* 15, no. 1 (2005), 14-21.

In the quest for optimal hip function, a normal amount of hip flexion is required. As testing for this standard will surely reveal, many runners fall far short of meeting the requirement of balanced, powerful hip function. If you train frequently, run frequently, and/or spend a significant amount of time sitting each day, your tissues can shorten and rob you of a normal degree of hip flexion, which in turn deteriorates your overall hip function. Power loss and the potential for injury go up.

In the 1970s, '80s, and '90s, the conventional thinking was that running injuries were directly associated with the feet. But this tide began to turn when researchers began to study hip function. Research conducted in 2002—comparing 30 runners suffering from chronic injuries with 30 runners who were healthy—looked at the level of strength and balance of six different muscles groups in the hips.[12] One of the things the researchers noted was that the injured runners had weak hip flexors and abductors.

That was just the beginning. Since then, research tracing injuries and excessive pronation to weak, tight hips has piled up.

If you're in the midst of trying to learn a new running technique, like the Pose Method, you'll want to attend to all of the standards related to hip function—squatting, hip flexion, hip extension, and ankle range of motion—to safely facilitate the change.

KEY MOTIVATION

Developing and/or maintaining proper hip flexion contributes to the healthy hip function, which will enable you to run with good form and balance and channel power from your posterior chain.

recommended mobility exercises for hip flexion

Unlock your hips by hammering yourself with lots of these:

- Banded Hip, Single-Leg Squat (page 231)
- Double-Band Hip Distraction (page 232)
- Glute Smash & Floss (page 235)
- Hamstring Smash (page 225) and Floss (page 224)

BRIEFING

One of the benefits of possessing normal range of motion and function in your hips is that it makes it a lot easier to move from one good position to another good position.

A good way to think of running is the way suggested by Dr. Nicholas Romanov, creator of the Pose Method. When gravity has brought you into contact with the ground in the midst of a foot strike, your body is in a "pose." You want to be in the best pose, or position, possible in terms of your lean, your posture, and the physics of where your body mass is in relationship to gravity. What follows is the movement to your next foot strike and a new pose on the opposite foot.

Put on your physicist's cap and think about all the various forces involved, in particular what goes into achieving stability in each new position of balancing on one leg, over and over and over. If it sounds easy, it isn't. Just ask any robotics engineer who's tried to build a machine that walks like a human.

Since I am mad for performance, I want you to seek the positions and motor patterns that lead to increased efficiency and minimize negative stresses.

To facilitate optimal patterns of movement in your running, you really need your hips in business and firing all thrusters. When you're running, a lack of hip extension or hip flexion forces you to make mechanical compromises downstream to generate the stability you need as you shift from pose to pose.

I address hip *extension* in Chapter 9. This standard addresses hip *flexion*.

Wait a second, you might think. *Aren't I practicing hip flexion all the time when I sit in my Aeron chair?*

You sure are. In fact, our bodies tend to mold themselves into the positions in which we spend the most time. If you spend hours every day in the sitting position, indeed, you're in a state of hip flexion.

Unfortunately, the hip flexion that occurs when you sit in a chair is short of the range needed to fulfill what the American Academy of Orthopedic Surgeons (AAOS) calls normal. If you're sitting up straight and tall, you're at 90 degrees. That's about 30 degrees short of where you need to be. If you're slumping in the chair, borrow your kid's protractor and see for yourself how short you're coming up. *Short* is a good word—being in the sitting position creates shortness in the hip capsule and the associated tissues of the hip, like the psoas.

The AAOS says that 120 degrees gets you a passing grade of normal.

> *Our bodies tend to mold themselves into the positions in which we spend the most time.*

death by sitting: your counterattack

Super ultramarathoner Dean Karnazes has managed to run across the country, run on a treadmill for two days straight, and finish epic races like the 135-mile Badwater Ultramarathon many times over. Injuries? Dean doesn't have time for injuries. One of his secrets, he says, is this:

"I rarely sit down."

Rather, Dean cultivates a habit of using a standing desk for his time on the computer and keeps the amount of time he spends sitting to an extreme minimum. He even breaks up his time standing at his computer with occasional blasts of air squats, push-ups, and pull-ups.

Not all of us are in a position to abandon the chair in favor of a standing desk. If that's the boat you're sailing on, use the bracing sequence (see page 65) to help set yourself for sitting with a braced neutral spine.

Every 15 minutes or so, get up out of your chair, shake things out, and go through the bracing sequence. With your pelvis reset and your spine organized, keep your butt and ab muscles on at about 20 percent tension and resume your seat.

NOTE: There's no shortcut for the bracing sequence. If you find yourself slumping in your chair, there's no effective way to recapture a braced neutral spine while seated. Pop up to your feet and redo your bracing sequence. Do it throughout your day, and over time you will have blown back tons of muscle-shortening damage that sitting would normally do to you.

In the test for this standard, I want you to accomplish a couple of different things:

- You will perform the test while standing in order to test your functionality with a small dose of load and balance work.
- You need to be able to demonstrate normal flexion in each hip.

You've passed the standard when you can maintain sufficient, 120-degree hip flexion for 30 seconds, standing on one leg and then repeating with the other leg.

This isn't just a test, of course, but an exercise in balance. If you're going to count on your legs and hips to generate copious amounts of stability as you run 3 miles, 10 miles, or more, it's a good idea to have the symphony of your motor control units, nervous pathways, and reflexes tuned. After you've mastered 30 seconds, add a challenge by closing your eyes.

1. Standing on one leg with a braced neutral spine and your feet straight, pull one knee to your chest to fully flex your hip.
2. Allow your hands to drop. To pass the standard, your knee must break the plane of the top of your hip and achieve a 120-degree angle of flexion or better.
3. Why not work on your plantar flexion, too? Point your toes. Hold this position for 30 seconds, and then repeat with the other leg for 30 seconds.

FAULT. You want to hold a tall position of stability. Pitching all over the sea doesn't make for a successful test of this standard.

Runner to Runner

Like many of the standards, hip flexion is a component of healthy hip function. Running lots of miles shorts most, if not all, of these components, and in the CrossFit classes I've attended, I've seen how much damage my running career (combined with a profession in which I sit a lot) has done. As much as I've improved in these areas, just about everyone else in the class has much better hip flexion and extension than I have. As you work toward the hip flexion standard, I encourage you to be creative in chasing down whatever might be impeding your range. For me, discovering that my psoas—the large muscles that run from the lower lumbar spine through the groin and flex the hip—are so short and tight from running and sitting that they've been the lock I never even thought of trying to turn.

As Kelly says, his mobility program is more of an open-source-code type of method. Take what he presents, play around with the techniques, and do your own explorations. Test a standard like this one, then perform a mobility exercise for two minutes, and then get up and retest. If you see a change, you know you're on to something.

—TJM

CHAPTER 9
STANDARD #6: HIP EXTENSION

Q: Do you have a normal amount of hip extension?

Meeting this standard means that you have enough range of motion in the front of your hips that you can press your hips into full extension.

KEY MOTIVATION

Taking care of your quads and hip flexors promotes healthy hip function and marginalizes the demonic forces that can torture your knees.

recommended mobility exercises for hip extension

Find time to do the Couch Stretch every day or, even better, several times a day.

- Couch Stretch (page 114)
- Banded Hip, Single-Leg Squat (page 231)
- Psoas Smash & Floss (page 234)

BRIEFING

For many runners, the front of the hip, or anterior hip, is a huge patch of trouble. This standard may be challenging for you to meet, depending on how much disarray your hips are in, but if you lay down focused and consistent work toward meeting this standard, you will reap tremendous rewards. Your hip function will improve, your posture will improve, and this may be the key to freeing you from the standard knee problems.

Here's a not-that-unique true story:

A 40-something runner with two decades of running, racing, and various wear-and-tear lines up for a half-marathon.[13] It's a surprisingly hilly course on the streets near downtown Los Angeles. Thirteen miles later, he tenderly crosses the finish line. As he hobbles his way through the post-race area looking to pick up his pre-race belongings transported by semi-trailer, he notices pain sizzling beneath both of his kneecaps. *Sizzle* is a good word, because he says that it felt like compressed chemical fires smoldering.

The burning worsened. He looked for relief by sitting down on a curb and rubbing his knees. It didn't help. Eventually the pain subsided, but joint pain of that intensity is a stark reflection of soft tissues and joints being exposed to destructive amounts of friction. This photo of the runner was taken about a half-mile from the finish of the race. It wasn't pretty. He right leg was reaching out, and his heel was smashing into the ground, with a locked-out knee absorbing the punishment from a gruesome heel strike. Was it any wonder that his knees felt like they were on fire?

I like car analogies, and this is one of my favorites: A runner who doesn't take care of business when it comes to poor movement patterns and the consequential shortening of the quadriceps and hip flexors is doing the equivalent of playing gas-o-brake-o with a car. Keep one foot on the brake

[13] As in *Ready to Run* co-author T.J. Murphy in 2010.

while you jam the other down on the gas pedal, and then, when the RPMs are hot, let go of the brake, sending the car lurching forward like a rocket. Then repeat. Do this long enough and you'll set the wheels on fire.

Knee pain is the most common chronic injury pain that runners confront, and a lot of the blame can be assigned to the freakishly short and tight muscles responsible for extending the leg. It can reveal itself in subtle ways.

At running shoe stores around the country, the gait test is a popular way to try to assess your biomechanical tendencies in hopes of matching you up with the right shoe. You might hop on a treadmill or head down the sidewalk for a series of short runs. The shoe salesman watching you often sees a peculiar pattern. Sometimes it's subtle, and sometimes it's not so subtle.

What he sees is this: As you plant one foot on the ground, the other foot has swung forward to become the new position of support. In the path of this movement—from leaving the ground behind to re-establishing contact with the ground, your leg swings your foot forward. The kink that the running shoe guy sees is in the way your foot rotates outward and your foot/leg operates in the manner of a Ping-Pong paddle. Rather than a direct path—your foot and leg remaining in a straight, neutral alignment throughout—this spinning-open movement looks as if you were trying to avoid slamming your toe into a brick sticking up out of the pavement, and your foot is taking the long way around the obstacle.

If you want to see how common this tic is, just spend some time in the pack of a big road race, and you'll see a virtual epidemic. What's going on here?

This is what's going on: If you are looping with your foot, you are missing one or more elements of good, powerful hip function. The muscle tissues at the front of your hip, the hip flexor and quads, are short, tight, and mashed up, which robs you of proper hip extension and the ability to maintain internal rotation of your upper leg. This lack of internal

A lot of the blame for knee pain can be assigned to the freakishly short and tight muscles responsible for extending the leg.

rotation effectively spills open your pelvis, and you end up dragging your leg around from foot plant to foot plant.

This spillage of stability and power has repercussions throughout your entire running system. It's a red carpet for the open-foot/knee-cave sequence that gives your joints an ugly twist of shear with every footfall.

This surrender of good hip function stresses the tissues in your knees and ankles, which take an ugly beating every time you go running. If you're holding a cadence of 160 steps per minute, that's more than 1,200 steps, or duty cycles, taken per mile if you're holding an 8-minutes-per-mile pace. You can do some more math with that: If you run 50 miles per week, 50 weeks a year, and you average 8 minutes per mile, we're talking about more than 3 million lashes of the razor whip.

Shoes and orthotics are not going to fix this problem, and it should be considered a death knell for your future as a healthy runner.

You must restore proper extension and internal rotation to your hips. You must restore it now and again and again and again. If you sit a lot throughout the day, then working toward achieving and maintaining this standard is going to require extra vigilance; you're going to have to build in a new set of habits.

I offer two primary weapons for you to use in the war on sitting:

- **Sit as little as possible.** (See the sidebar "Why Sitting Really Is Hell on Square Wheels" on page 116.)
- **Do the Couch Stretch every day.** This stretch is to healthy running what flossing is to healthy teeth.

THE COUCH STRETCH

The Couch Stretch is a weapons-grade technique to open up the hip and open up some slack upstream of the knee. It can help alleviate some of the common types of knee pain that runners confront, like patella tendinitis (aka runner's knee), and help resolve hip and back pain. Meeting this standard will support your mission to sustain good posture both in your running and as you go about your day.

Back your feet up against a wall, a box, or the upper cushion of your couch. If you're on a hard floor, put down a cushion for your knee.

Slide your left leg so that your knee fits into the corner where the floor meets the wall (or whatever corner you're using). Make your shin flush with the wall and point your toe.

IMPORTANT: Squeeze your glutes, in particular your left glute. Keep squeezing throughout the mobilization. This will stabilize your lower back and position your hip joint correctly.

Draw up your right leg and post it in front of you, with your shin vertical.

TIP: If you're too tight to get into the Couch Stretch position, scale it back by positioning a box in front of you. Put your weight on the box and don't worry about posting your leg, as in step 3. Work at this daily for at least two minutes on each side to effect the tissue change that you need to improve toward the unmodified position and meet this standard.

With your butt squeezed, drive the front of your hip toward the ground. Maintain this position for at least one minute.

Really crank your hip flexor by lifting your torso (with your glutes still engaged) and hold for another minute.

Drive your torso upright, with your glutes and abdominals engaged.

why sitting really is hell on square wheels

To support good hip extension and overall hip function, don't limit your work on this standard to four minutes of mobility work per day. You need to overhaul the habits that do the damage.

If you've read a book like *Born to Run* or *Running with the Kenyans,* you have learned that ethereal spirits like the Tarahumara Indians from northern Mexico and the runners from the Rift Valley in Kenya have a few things in common. For one thing, rather than jump into the VW to get to school or drop off the dry cleaning, they run everywhere for transport. Getting dinner means either farming or hunting on foot. Then, at night, the Tarahumaras like to throw a beer bash and drink and dance until dawn, and then they go out and do some more running the next day.

Contrast this with a day in the life of the average American. The first stop is sitting at a breakfast table over a bowl of Wheaties. The second stop is sitting in a car, bus, or train for the commute to work or school. Work or school is usually a festival of more sitting, broken up with occasional breaks. Then the commute home—more sitting—and then dinner, and then maybe it's time to sink into the couch for an episode or two of *Survivor.*

If there's one critical takeaway from this book, it's that every minute you spend sitting is a minute spent with your hips turned off and positioned in a state of lazy flexion. Your hip flexors shorten as a result, and all that tremendous power that you should be funneling into your running gets diminished to a trickle.

I want you to adopt a warrior stance when it comes to the amount of time you spend sitting each day. Cultivate an awareness that each minute you tick off sitting is doing damage to your body and to your running. When you can, avoid sitting, or even open up a direct attack. Set your phone or watch timer to go off every hour so that you get up out of your chair, mobilize for a minute or two, and then (if you have to go back to sitting) sit down with your butt and stomach muscles turned on and engaged.

Runner to Runner

You know that quad stretch that you've probably done while waiting for a stoplight to turn green during a run? One hand goes on the pole, the other hand grabs your foot and pulls the quad into a stretch via a flexed leg. Okay, go ahead and do that, and then commit yourself to two minutes in the Couch Stretch position.

I think the difference between what these two movements feel like and what they accomplish is perhaps the best answer to the question "Why mobilize and not just stretch?" or the question "What's the difference between mobilizing and stretching?" The Couch Stretch, when performed correctly, is not just horrifically uncomfortable for a tight-as-a-banjo runner; it's a guide through the depths of ball-and-socket anatomy. You become familiar with the deeper tissues around your hip joint as the exercise helps you work toward proper position of the femur in the hip capsule. The quad-pull stretch is easier to do, but it just doesn't pack any punch. If I had to choose only one mobility exercise to do from this book, it would probably be the Couch Stretch. It put an end to my knee troubles.

—TJM

CHAPTER 10
STANDARD #7: ANKLE RANGE OF MOTION

Q: Do you have normal range of motion in your ankles?

To achieve this standard, you need to be able to express a normal range of ankle motion with a dose of bodyweight load—in other words, be able to kneel and hold the pistol position with either leg.

KEY MOTIVATION

Unglued ankles enable you to move with optimal patterns and access the full, free power of elastic recoil for your running.

recommended mobility exercises for ankle range of motion

Your feet and ankles are amazing spring-like mechanisms that offer tremendous quantities of elastic recoil. To open them up, work on these mobilizations:

- Plantar Mobilizations (page 217)
- Dorsiflexion Work (page 218)
- Plantar Flexion Overdrive (page 219)
- Anterior Hip Smash (page 223)
- Couch Stretch (page 114)

BRIEFING

Meeting this standard is going to seem like an insurmountable challenge to many runners. Because runners' lower legs take considerable abuse, most runners who drop into a yoga class for the first time struggle just to point their toes; the image of the foot being pressed by body weight into a position of full plantar flexion sends up a pain chill. Chalk this up to being a fact of the running life. But a lack of range of motion in your ankle joints won't just earn you frowns in yoga class. In a runner, it is expressed in the turned-out duck-foot position (see Chapter 4), valgus knee collapse, collapsed arches, plantar fascia stress, bone spurs, bunions, and—it almost goes without saying—injury pain that threatens to turn the runner into a former runner.

Because it is the center of such strife for runners, I'm going to talk specifically about the heel cord, but first I'd like to frame the ankle joint and the surrounding fascias (connective tissues), bones, and muscles as a system. Within this system lies the connection between the leaf spring–like mechanism of your feet and arches to your lower leg bones.

The Achilles tendon, or what we often call the heel cord, is a 6-inch stretch of tendon that attaches the calf muscles to the heel bone. It's so tough that you could use it to suspend a Ford Fiesta above the ground.

Yet, as another testament to the way distance runners can put on the blinders and dutifully fill up the logbook from the awakening of spring to the darkest depths of winter, the degeneration into a state of chronic tendonosis is not uncommon. Despite the amazing capacity of the heel cord, running lots of miles and running fast tend to stiffen it up—even more so if you've been running in shoes with steep drops and with your knees caving inward, rolling through collapsed arches, and pulling your heel cords off the vertical axis.

The Achilles tendon is so tough that you could use it to suspend a Ford Fiesta.

Add to your running mileage the following punishers:

- The 10,000 or so steps that you take in a day
- Any stress that you might channel through the conduits in the weight room
- The price that's been exacted if you've spent considerable time in shoes with elevated heels
- Your entire posterior chain being out of sorts because you're slumped in an office chair eight hours a day

This chain of problems can be expressed in debilitating knee pain.

You know the saying that there are no bad dogs, only bad dog owners? The same has been said about runners and other athletes in regard to tissues like the heel cord. There are no bad heel cords, only bad heel cord owners. When the ankle and heel cord are treated poorly, the repercussions can and will be felt up and down the kinetic chain.

There are no bad heel cords, only bad heel cord owners.

In consistently working toward and maintaining this standard, I want you to embrace becoming the good-dog-owner type.

By encouraging you to pursue the ankle range of motion standard, I am primarily coaxing you to strive for and maintain a healthy, functional, and elastic ankle complex. If you're a runner with some solid numbers on the odometer and you haven't been performing regular maintenance on your feet and ankles, then meeting this standard is going to take some work and some patience.

So let's start at the beginning. I imagine that if you're reading this book, you want to

- Become a better runner.
- Make running a regular part of your training program.
- Run better in the service of your sport or profession.

- Make a return to running from the chaos of injury.
- Ensure as best you can that you will enjoy running for the rest of your life.

You're the reason I put this book together. And making a daily habit of working toward normal range of motion in your ankles and feet is going to help you achieve these goals.

In the running world, it is widely accepted that stiff, immobile ankles are one of costs of doing business. But the real cost is performance. If you are limited in either plantar flexion (pointing your toe) or dorsiflexion (flexing your foot), then you are leaving a big pile of gold coins on the table in terms of the capacity to use the movement patterns you were born to use and the elastic recoil that translates to power and speed over lengthy spans of road and trail.

The value of elastic recoil for a runner made for one of my favorite scenes in the movie *Gallipoli,* when the young Aussie sprinter, Archy, gets coached by his uncle.

> Uncle: What are your legs?
> *Archy: Springs. Steel springs.*
> What are they going to do?
> *Hurl me down the track.*
> How fast can you run?
> *As fast as a leopard.*
> How fast are you going to run?
> *As fast as a leopard!*
> Then let's see you do it!

That's right: as fast as a leopard. But if the springs have been transmogrified into tourniquets and have become part of the stability-shoe-as-a-plaster-cast system, then this isn't going to happen. Poor ankle range of motion is also a side effect of wearing shoes that elevate your heels (as discussed in Chapter 5).

Here's the good news: Your tissues can change, your joints can change, and you can change.

But it's not going to happen overnight. Making the appropriate changes to your tissues and joints takes consistent, steady attention over days, weeks, and months. There is no magic pill, and a weekend workshop alone is at best going to put you on the right path.

Pursuing the ankle range of motion standard means committing to a journey similar to that of transforming your physiology to be aerobically prepared to run a marathon. It's going to take the same brand of work ethic and patience.

The path is committing at least 15 minutes per day to the work of repositioning your joints, restoring the glide between the sliding surfaces in your tissues, and improving your movement patterns.

Obsessed with performance? Then daily routine maintenance on your feet and ankles needs to become an obsession as well.

To meet this standard, you'll need to pass the following two tests. Both tests insert a dose of load so that you get true insight into the functionality of your ankles. Double win: Passing these tests also requires healthy hip function.

Your tissues can change, your joints can change, and you can change.

TEST #1: DORSIFLEXION

Can you get into the pistol position? The pistol is a full-flexion single-leg squat.

Start in a standing position with your feet together.

Drive your knees outward as you lower your butt toward the ground.

Rounding your back is okay, but keep your heels on the ground. The focus is on ankle flexion.

With your butt lowered, prepare to extend your right leg into the pistol position.

This is the complete pistol position. Notice how the left leg is in full flexion, the heel is on the ground, and the knee is tracking in line with the foot.

COLLAPSED-FOOT FAULT. When the arch collapses, the knee goes with it.

TEST #2: PLANTAR FLEXION

Can you get into a kneeling position?

1. This is it: a full kneeling position with both feet in dorsiflexion. As fascia expert Jill Miller will tell you, spending time in this position will do wonders for the battered and shortened fascia within your feet and around your ankles. Don't be surprised if you start sweating even though you're still.
2. To pass the kneeling test, your feet must be in full dorsiflexion and straight.

Runner to Runner

Ready to Run is meant to be a bridge for a runner besieged with injury problems and power outages to a state in which the body can run the way it was designed to run. Part of getting to the end state is addressing running form. You've probably heard of some of the programs available, the Pose Method being the one that started it all. By working toward and ideally meeting the 12 *Ready to Run* standards, you will put your body in a good position to take on this exceptionally valuable, yet often complicated transformation.

One of the potholes for a lot of runners converting from a heel strike to a forefoot strike is the different form of stress on the ankle complex. I experienced it myself the first time I tried Pose Running drills while migrating toward a CrossFit Endurance approach to running. My heel cords had been short for some time. The Pose drills call on the feet and lower legs to behave like thick-coiled springs, and elasticity of these springs becomes a primary currency of running. But if you lack range of motion in your ankles and your heel cords are weakened from the kind of atrophy that comes with heel-striking, it can be too much. After four weeks of drills, I was enjoying major progress—I had adapted to a faster cadence and the trip hammer–like action that the running form uses. So I started doing more and more of it. That put too much stress on my left ankle, and I ended up with a hotspot that took several weeks to cool down.

My suggestion is to prepare. If you're going to make the commitment to change your running form, really have this standard and the Jumping and Landing standard dialed in. As Dr. Nicholas Romanov, the scientist who defined the Pose Method, told me in an interview, "You have to have complete commitment." So it's probably best to start your running drills very slowly—drilling once or twice a week max—and allow your body to progressively adapt to the new stress. As Kelly says, tissues have the capacity to change, but it takes time. Let your heel cords strengthen with the work.

If you attend a weekend workshop to learn a new running technique, go in with patience. It's the rare runner indeed who is going to be able to turn his or her running technique inside out in two days and never look back. Brian MacKenzie's CrossFit Endurance website has a guide to preparing for a weekend seminar: www.crossfitendurance.com/seminarprep. (MacKenzie teaches the Pose Method at his CFE seminars.) It may take you up to a year to fully ingrain the new movement patterns. Starting with good hip function, adequate range of motion throughout your body, and strong, supple ankles will make a huge difference.

—TJM

CHAPTER 11
STANDARD #8: WARMING UP AND COOLING DOWN

Q: Do you routinely perform pre-run warm-ups and post-run cool-downs?

Even if your schedule is already crushed, you need to make warming up and cooling down a priority for every run and figure out a way to do it *every time*.

KEY MOTIVATION

Athletes who run often give short shrift to warm-ups and cool-downs. Or they discard them completely. But by making a concentrated effort to perform a solid warm-up and cool-down before and after each and every workout that includes running, you'll gain tremendous injury prevention and accelerated recovery benefits.

recommended mobility exercises for warm-ups and cool-downs

Air squats (page 92) and jumping rope are potent exercises to help you warm up your joints and tissues. Use your cool-down time to work on your mobility weaknesses—or you can always hit the reset button with these favorites:

- Couch Stretch (page 114)
- Hip Capsule Rotation (page 237)
- Spending time in a deep squat

BRIEFING

We are all mad for performance. It's in this madness that the passion and fun of being an athlete lives. In rating yourself on this standard, take a good look at how much of this passion and willingness to push yourself in a workout—be it a tempo run, a grueling MetCon, or a soccer scrimmage—you are funneling toward a thorough warm-up and a thorough cool-down.

I've traveled to nearly every continent teaching courses in human performance and mechanics in every imaginable athletic setting, from universities to CrossFit gyms to professional and national team facilities to military performance centers. Most of these gyms are stocked with a plenitude of foam rollers. And before a group workout starts, I'll see a few of the athletes lying around on the floor, haphazardly using the rollers, in stark contrast to the several others who are going just as hard at their warm-ups as they will in the workout. They jump rope, perform mobility work to prepare their joints and various muscle groups for the workout of the day, and work on their weak spots.

You see the same duality at a triathlon team track workout. Some athletes stand on the infield, chatting with friends, hanging out, and waiting for the start time. Others are actively performing running drills, mobilizing, and performing full-body functional movements like lunges and burpees to get their tissues hot and their circulatory systems moving.

Training is also about how you prepare for a workout and how you close it out.

Training is not about the workout alone. It's also about how you prepare for the workout and how you close it out. You train to make your body stronger, faster, more durable, and better able to sustain long efforts. You train to incur these sorts of physical adaptations within your body. To meet this standard, you need to think beyond the 6 x 800s on the track, or how fast you can perform five rounds of a 400-meter run and 15 overhead squats (the CrossFit workout known as Nancy). It's about thinking of yourself as an athlete around the clock:

- How well are you hydrating throughout the day?
- Are you getting enough sleep?
- Are you sitting as little as possible, and when you do sit, are you working in short spurts of mobility work to counter the effects?

And it's about making time to do an appropriate warm-up before every workout and a thorough cool-down after every workout. If you put your energy into a hard training effort but do little beforehand and nothing afterward to maximize the benefits of that training, or to do it in a way that doesn't shred your tissues, then you aren't netting a full return on your hard-fought investment. You won't achieve the full amount of adaptation that you could, and the injury risk factor gets ratcheted up as well.

Does the driver of a Formula 1 race car just buckle up and smash the pedal to the floor? Does the winning jockey in the Kentucky Derby cross the finish line with his horse and then hop right out of the saddle? Of course not. With the Ferrari F14 T, the driver uses an external heater to warm up the engine before he even thinks of hitting the ignition. Cooling down a horse? This is what *Trainer Magazine* has to say:

> "The aim of a cool-down period is a progressive reduction in exercise intensity allowing a gradual redistribution of blood flow, enhanced lactic acid removal from the muscles, and a reduction of body heat through convection and evaporation. If a horse is inadequately cooled after competing, any residual lactate in the system will affect performance if the horse is required to compete again within a short space of time. The application of cold water will result in heat loss by conduction from the skin to the water, thus reducing body temperature. The active cool-down will also result in an effective return to normal breathing and heart rate."[14]

[14] "The importance of warm-up and cool-down in the racehorse," *Trainer Magazine,* June 27, 2008, accessed via http://trainermagazine.com/published-articles/2013/8/8/the-importance-of-warm-up-and-cool-down-in-the-racehorse

Contrast these images with a lunch-hour run. It's a time-challenged situation—you have to blast your way from work to a place to change into your training clothes and then to wherever you're going to run, do your workout, and then rush to be back on the job. In this situation, a prioritization process takes place, and the warm-up and cool-down often get tossed. They are taken for granted as unaffordable luxuries.

This gets to the problem that modern athletes living in the post-agricultural/post-industrial information age face. Except for an hour or so when we have time to train, most of us live in a sedentary fashion—a lifestyle we aren't designed for. From the viewpoint of evolution and biology, our bodies were engineered for long periods of walking and lots of moving around to survive. But in modern civilization—except for that run or trip to the gym—we're physically lethargic. When we work, when we're in the car or on the bus, and when we're having dinner, we are sedentary.

Here's a scenario that's probably going to sound familiar: You have a morning run workout scheduled, and you wake up, drink some coffee, and go at it, figuring that you'll warm up as you get going into the session. The problem is that you're trying to warm up by hammering the pavement with cold joints, connective tissues, and muscles, and with no "oil" running through your system. It might seem like you're getting away with something, but consider this: If it is 5:00 a.m. and your beloved Ferrari has been sitting outside in the cold all night, are you just going to turn on the ignition and hit the gas and hope that the drive to the freeway on-ramp is enough to warm it up without any strain?

The worst thing you can do after you finish a workout is to sit your butt down in a chair for a long time. You've put in a big dose of stimulation, and then you pull up to your desk. Sitting brings muscle contractions to a halt, and muscle contractions are what help clear congestion out of your system. Sitting shuts down the recovery mechanisms that are critical to your training adaptations. Your circulation is compromised, and so is your lymphatic system. It's like tying knots in a bunch of garden hoses.

Here's my message: Your muscles, fascias, ligaments, tendons, cartilage, and nerves deserve the same amount of obsession as a race car or racehorse, if not way more.

You're already strapped for time. So what can you do? If you commit yourself to ritualizing warm-ups and cool-downs, you're halfway there.

Your muscles, fascias, ligaments, tendons, cartilage, and nerves deserve the same amount of obsession as a race car or racehorse, if not way more.

WARMING UP

Every time you work out, start with a few minutes of walking to get your blood flowing. Follow that with some dynamic, nonlinear, full-body movements, like arm circles, lunges, and burpees. Take two minutes to mobilize any high-priority joints or range of motion issues with a mobility exercise or two from Part 3 of this book. One last useful measure is to do some quick jump-rope work. Jumping rope is great for:

- **Strengthening your feet**
- **Waking up your foot strike**
- **Jump-starting your heart and getting the fluids moving within your body**
- **Heating up the precious soft tissues within your feet and around your ankles that extend into your calves**

COOLING DOWN

Don't finish your workout at warp 8 and then transition like a triathlete through a shower into your business suit and sink into an executive recliner for the rest of the day. Instead, here's a power move you can do: Turn the last half-mile of your run into a walk. Imagine that you own Seabiscuit, and you're protecting your cherished investment. While you walk, do some leg swings, arm swings, trunk rotations, and the like to maximize the benefits.

If that's all the cooling down you have time for, that's all you have time for, and that alone is fantastic. If you can add five minutes of mobility work with a lacrosse ball, roller, or other mobilization tool in order to get in some work on one of the other standards, that's even better.

Then spend as much of the rest of the day as you can drinking fluids and being an athlete rather than sitting. Beware the chair. If you do have to sit, get up and reset yourself with the bracing sequence (see page 65) as often as possible. Throw in the occasional mobility minute when you can.

Here are some good cool-downs. I recommend 10 to 15 minutes for these, but if five minutes is what you have, then five minutes it is:

- **An easy 10 to 15 minutes on a rowing machine**
- **An easy bike ride around the neighborhood**
- **A walk—barefoot if possible**
- **A selection of bodyweight movements, like lunges, jumping jacks, and arm and leg circles**

THE ACCORDION

The amount of warming up and cooling down you do needs to increase when your workout involves greater intensity.

I've got one last note for you on warming up and cooling down. You probably already understand this one, but it's worth underscoring: The amount of warming up and cooling down you do needs to increase when your workout involves greater intensity.

Let's say that your training session consists of 6 x 800 meters on the track at your 5k race pace. It's a tough workout, both physically and psychologically. Fully preparing your systems for the jolt of the first rep might require 30 to 45 minutes. If you're a Masters runner and/or you have an injury rap sheet that you'd rather not think about, definitely aim for the higher number of warm-up minutes. Warm up like a sprinter. Sprinters may race for only 10 or 20 seconds, but their warm-ups and cool-downs are long and involved processes. A good sprinter knows full well that he or she isn't going to be at full speed without a hard, no-stone-unturned warm-up and a coolant-flush warm-down.

This inverse relationship between the time you spend warming up and the duration of a race or other competition is a key principle to embrace: The shorter the event, the more speed and power required, the more warm-up. A CrossFit athlete waiting for the clock to start on high-octane workout like Fran would be wise to spend a lot more time warming up than a CrossFit athlete about to start Murph.[15] Similarly, the amount of warm-up you're going to require before a flat road marathon is very different from the amount you might need before a 3-mile cross-country race on a roller-coaster course.

For hard, high-intensity training, it's best to make sure that you have more than 5 minutes for your warm-up and more than 5 minutes for your cool-down. It would be much better to have 20 minutes on either side of any hard anaerobic effort.

[15] Fran consists of 21-15-9 reps of thrusters and pull-ups. The world's best CrossFitters finish it in 2 to 3 minutes. Murph is a 1-mile run, 100 pull-ups, 200 push-ups, 300 squats, and another 1-mile run, all while wearing a 20-pound weight vest, and it takes most athletes at least an hour to perform.

CHAPTER 12
STANDARD #9: COMPRESSION

Q: Are you wearing compression socks?

For more than half a century, doctors have been prescribing compression for patients who need a boost in their blood circulation. The first compression socks may have been designed for people battling varicose veins, but this doesn't mean that they won't benefit you as an athlete.

KEY MOTIVATION

Compression is a relatively easy and effective way to assist your body's circulation and lymphatic systems in restoring worked tissue.

BRIEFING

There isn't much detail to this standard. It boils down to this: You're an athlete. And the starting wide receiver for the Green Bay Packers is an athlete. He has access to a world-class training staff and every technology on the market to help him recover from training, practice, and the trauma of the many game-day collisions that are part of his life. You don't have the same access to a training room staff, but you still take a pounding from your running (in no way similar to life in the NFL, but hey, it's still a pounding). One thing you can afford?

Compression socks will do you good. Buy a pair and wear them as often and as consistently as possible.

Compression socks. Wearing compression socks doesn't require a lot of time, and it really doesn't cost that much money. And it works. You're buried in commitments, and you may not have the time or money for a weekly massage, but compression socks will do you good. Buy a pair and wear them as often and as consistently as possible.

Imagine this scenario: After nine months of training for the NYC Marathon, you board a 757 for a flight from Phoenix to JFK Airport and shoehorn yourself into the window seat. You bunch up a jacket and cram it against the hull to serve as a pillow, trying to sleep. When make your first move to deplane, you feel as if you're being extracted from a crashed car. It takes the better part of the next few hours to feel your legs again.

The race begins the next morning on the Verrazano Bridge. With 48,000 other runners, you tour 26.2 miles of the five boroughs and cross the finish line in Central Park. The celebration begins. Eventually, a margarita appears in your hand.

The next day, you fold yourself into another window seat on another plane, the vessel climbs to cruising altitude, and you head for home. Your legs are throbbing from the 26.2-mile effort. But the race is over now, so what?

As I'm sure you picked up on, if you were this runner, you put your body through the ringer. Most athletes know that flying accelerates dehydration, and that carrying a water bottle (better to spike that water with salts—see page 162) and getting up whenever possible during the flight to assist your body's blood and lymph systems keeps things moving into, out of, and around your cells.

What I see in otherwise highly disciplined athletes when they travel for a big event is a failure to think about the needs of their tissues and their internal chemistry. Answering those needs will make for not only a better tomorrow, but a better future in general. After a race has blown your tissues to hell, it is more important than ever to eat nutritious meals; rehydrate;

spend time moving, massaging, and rolling your tissues; and get good rest to let your systems do their repair work.

Failure to maintain this kind of discipline can be seen during the average week in some athletes. For example, the worst thing you can do after tearing through your morning run is to race off to work and sit all day. (You'll notice that this point comes up throughout this book.) Why? Because sitting shuts down the lymph system and brings your body's cellular cleaning and repair systems to a cold stop.

I get it, though: You have only so much time. Squeezing in a one-hour run is not easy. This standard is meant as a time-efficient helper for time-stressed runners, and it's a simple one to implement.

Use compression socks. Strategize a solution for wearing them at least some of the time every day.

While there is debate about whether compression wear is of any value while running, there's no valid argument against wearing a simple pair of compression socks after your daily workout or when you fly—two of the most critical times when compression will help you.

You can buy a pair of compression socks at your local running shoe store or online for about $25. They're worth it. They're easy to use—just pull them on after a run or before you board a plane. Sure, you can opt for the full leggings or more, but all I'm asking for with this standard is that you make a habit of wearing compression *socks.* You can wear them under your business-casual clothes and generally avoid the dork factor that comes with compression wear. (If you wear your compression socks with Birkenstocks, you're on your own.)

Hopping on a transcontinental flight after a marathon? Wear as much compression apparel as you can get your hands on.

Compression is such a vital weapon in your arsenal, in fact, that it plays a major component in the next standard: stamping out tissue hotspots.

Runner to Runner

It's almost weird that a technology like compression for recovery is as controversial as it is. When it comes to supporting the notion that compression wear, worn while at rest, can improve blood flow and thus prod the recovery cycle of training, the research is solid.[16] Following the information that came through from the Byrne study, a runner would be prudent to shop for socks with compression of around 20 mmHg for optimal blood flow (mmHg, or millimeters of mercury, is a unit of pressure).

Although compression wear gets slammed by some critics, there's no doubt that runners, triathletes, and CrossFitters are using it in great numbers. It can't be considered a study by any measure, but each year that I flew across the Pacific to cover the Hawaii Ironman, I noticed an increasing percentage of the triathletes on board wearing compression socks. (It's always easy to spot the triathletes—sunglasses, race T-shirts, Ironman tattoos,

carry-on luggage in the shape of race wheels, men with shaved legs.) Triathletes have long been early adopters of new technologies—like aerodynamic handlebars—even if they look funny.

There's an additional occasion on which I've started wearing compression socks: immediately after any sort of high-intensity workout that involves running. I've always been prone to calf cramps after interval running and long race efforts—calf cramps that feel like someone has plunged a switchblade into my gastrocs. Any measure to prevent that feeling, be it nutrition, mobility work, or recovery techniques, I'm all for using.

—TJM

[16] Belinda Byrne, RN, "Deep vein thrombosis prophylaxis: The effectiveness and implications of using below-knee or thigh-length graduated compression stockings," *Heart and Lung* 30 (2001), 277-84.

CHAPTER 13
STANDARD #10: NO HOTSPOTS

Q: Are you free of hotspots of pain?

You are Ready to Run when your routine maintenance is up-to-date and you have no hot, sketchy tissues or joints.

KEY MOTIVATION

Staying a runner is the key motivation here—not having to trade in your morning run for reading the newspaper on the Lifecycle. Running through pain and injury has repercussions. There's no getting away with it: It is how you do more damage or wear things out for good. The benefit of fixing your hotspots is that you get to enjoy being a runner now and for years to come.

BRIEFING

Imagine that you're three months into a six-month training plan for a marathon in which you want to PR (set a personal record). You've been going at it hard, mixing in long runs, fast runs, and a few races: some local 5ks and 10ks to blow out the tubes.

It's been great. Your race times are improving, and your pace for your long runs is dropping. But you can't help but notice that a few annoying little pains are starting to crop up.

Your left heel burns during the first mile of a run. And there's a throbbing pain from deep in your right hip that haunts you after you finish a run.

A couple of weeks go by, and the pains seem to be sharpening rather than going away. They're getting worse. You're beginning to wonder if it's time to shift into cross-training mode or to go through the boring suffer-fest that is wearing a flotation belt and water-jogging in a pool.

You're in a running club, and in that club is an ultrarunning star. When some people think of ultramarathoning, they think of 50-mile runs, 100-kilometer trail races, or a 135-mile scorcher across Death Valley. The ultrarunner in your club does that, but even more: Once a year he jumps into a six-day race. The gun goes off, and whoever accumulates the most miles in six days wins. The guy on your team wins one of these things every year. So you figure—reasonably—that he must know something about defying injuries. Anyone who can run 160 miles a week in training and then run more than 110 miles a day for six days to win a race must have some otherworldly insight into how to evade injuries. So in a running shoe store where you happen to bump into him, you ask:

"What's your advice on dealing with injuries?"

The ultrarunner looks you in the eye the way a Jedi Master would, and then he gives you the answer:

"I'm not the right guy to talk to about that."

He goes on to explain that his mastery over injury has a lot to do with his ability to ignore injury pain. In other words, he just runs through it.

Sound familiar? As you dial in this standard, the first thing to acknowledge is how the average runner can tolerate discomfort. It is indeed a Jedi power: You're at mile 23 of a marathon, with 3 miles to go, and you're *in extremis* (Latin for "at the point of death"). Not only do you keep going, but you keep holding your goal race pace for 3.2 anguish-filled and never-ending miles. You have gone metaphysical.

But there's a dark side to this power: Runners and other athletes tend to wield it like a sword against the discomfort they encounter in races and in hard workouts, and it builds up a stubborn inner strength that unfortunately leads to ignoring the signal flares being sent from the depths of the body that damage is being done.

You have heel pain? Or your knee is dodgy? Or there's a stabbing pain in your butt? There's a mechanics problem or a dysfunction of some sort that is screaming to be taken care of.

Can you run through it? Temporarily, yes. Your body is amazing when it comes to meeting the demands that you place on it. To draw from another sci-fi domain, you are Captain Kirk, and your body is like Mr. Scott and the *Starship Enterprise.* Even if you've taken heavy damage from battle, if you tell Mr. Scott to find you more power and get you to hold warp 10, Mr. Scott will jerry-rig some energy pathway, even if it brings the rattling ship to the brink of exploding.

The body tends to have a failsafe mechanism, however, when you keep pushing and grinding your way past injuries. It will shut down. In the case of the six-day champion ultrarunner, this is exactly what happened. Struck by a bad case of piriformis sciatica (deep butt pain that can be felt down the leg), he put his head down and tried to run through it. His body shut down on him, and his running came to a prolonged stop.

The culture of running through pain and its badge-of-honor quality are interwoven into all sports that are categorized by the word *endurance.* When the athletic test revolves around how much can be endured, lines get crossed. Running through hotspots over months and years can lead to devastating consequences. Some of the more severe examples include peroneal tendon surgery in the ankle, the surgical removal of shredded knee cartilage, and hip replacement.

When you keep pushing and grinding your way past injuries, your body will shut down.

It's not just the badge-of-honor culture. It's that a runner doesn't want to give up the daily run. It's crazy how much damage a state of denial can throw down upon a joint that was meant to last 110 years. Consider this forum post from "Amanda D" on www.hiprunner.com, a website for runners who have had hip replacements:

> "I've been lying to myself and others about the pain for several months now. I believe my mental need to run has outweighed the physical pain of running for me for awhile. But I did finally go to an orthopedic surgeon (well, 3) last week, and all were shocked by my bone on bone osteoarthritis in my left hip and how I was walking (barely) let alone running."

As I said at the beginning of this book: I'm on your side. I want you to be able to run until your last days on Earth. But that's not going to happen if you fail to understand a fundamental rule when it comes to movement:

If you feel pain during or after moving, then what you were doing was not functional movement.

So while running is considered a compound, functional movement that we humans were designed to do in daily life, if you're feeling pain or limping with a hotspot, then you're doing something wrong.

As I like to say, if it feels sketchy, it is sketchy. If you have a gnawing sensation that you may be grinding up some soft tissue, guess what? You're probably grinding up some soft tissue. If you feel something burning, tearing, or becoming inflamed, it's time to take a few steps back and fix the problem.

The purpose of this standard is to get you to tune in and respond immediately to all of your body's signals. If your process has been to wait around until the pain or swelling becomes so bad that you think, *Oh no! I have to do something about this!*, then you've waited too long. It's like being a soldier in a firefight who waits for his M16 to jam before he realizes that he probably should have cleaned it recently.

FIXING HOTSPOTS

First of all, let's revisit running shoes and clear something out of the mindset. I talked about this earlier in the book, but it's worth mentioning again because it's so pervasive and automatic. For years, this has been an all-too-common program for dealing with running injuries:

1.   A runner goes running.
2.   The runner notices a tweak during the run. _____ starts hurting, and the hot, wincing pain gets worse as the run goes on.
3.   The runner still feels pain after the run. He gets out a bag of frozen peas, puts it on the hotspot, and tries to "stretch it out."
4.   The runner thinks, "I must need a different type of running shoe."

Here's a new model:

1.   The runner does a thorough warm-up before the run (see page 133), including mobility work to tend to areas in particular need (see Part 3).
2.   The runner notices a tweak during the run. _____ starts hurting, and the runner immediately cuts the run short.
3.   Back at home, the runner begins focused compression work on and near the hotspot. (See "VooDoo Floss Band compression to the rescue," coming up next.)

4. The runner performs mobilizations above and below the problem. This is as simple as it sounds—go after the tissue above and below the hotspot with the mobility exercises outlined in Part 3 of this book. Spend at least two minutes with each mobilization. If the hotspot is in your knee, for example, then you should perform mobilizations for your lower leg and upper thigh.

VooDoo Floss Band compression to the rescue

Compression is not just a tool for managing your ongoing recovery. When you tweak something and a joint swells up, compression is a dynamic aid that, if used correctly, will work wonders to restore range of motion and heal sticky sliding surfaces between tissues.

Let's say, for example, that your heel is sore and inflamed. At the heart of the *Ready to Run* approach is that I want you to dig into the underlying mechanics and repair the problem at its root. This may include some of the following measures:

- Restoring foot and arch strength
- Adapting to a flat shoe
- Improving your posture
- Improving the channel of force moving from your posterior chain

But that heel is also going to need some immediate attention. I want you to apply deep compression immediately above and below the hotspot.

I call this compression technique "VooDoo" because it attacks a swollen joint or dinged muscle in a broad spectrum of ways. You may not be sure *why* it worked, but you'll know that it worked.

Here are some of the ways VooDoo Floss Band compression can help you:

- It restores sliding surface function, creating an omnipotent shearing effect that unglues those sticky sliding surfaces.
- It restores range of motion to the joint.
- It floods the area with blood. When you release the band, blood floods in with nutrients. This is especially valuable for those connective tissues that don't easily get a lot of blood flow.
- It reduces swelling and revives the joint. When a joint is swollen, the natural stream of information from proprioceptors is lost, as nerve endings get dulled. Joint mechanics suffer. VooDoo Floss Band compression pushes swelling back into the lymphatic system.

VooDoo Floss Band compression technique

Be forewarned that VooDoo Floss Band compression isn't as enjoyable as a Swedish massage; it's on the uncomfortable side of things. But use common sense: If it hurts in a sketchy way, then it's sketchy.

Here's the essential method for using VooDoo Floss Band compression to manage a fresh hotspot:

1. Start a few inches below the hotspot.
2. Wrap the band toward your heart. If you're wrapping your knee, for example, start below the knee.
3. Use a half-inch overlap with each wrap of the band.
4. Shoot for about 75 percent of stretch tension when wrapping the problem spot. The areas above and below it can be at about 50 percent tension.
5. Leave a bit of slack as you near the finish so that you can tie off the band.
6. Once it's wrapped, immediately begin moving the joint or the entire limb through its full range of motion.
7. If you start to go numb in the area of the band, or if you feel pins and needles coming on, it's time to unwrap. This can happen in just two minutes.
8. After unwrapping, don't be alarmed if the hue of your skin makes you think of a cadaver. Normal flesh tone will return with the rush of fresh blood.

If you are using VooDoo Floss Band compression to restore sliding surfaces, two or three times per day is going to be plenty.

If you are using compression to counter swelling, then five to ten times per day is okay.

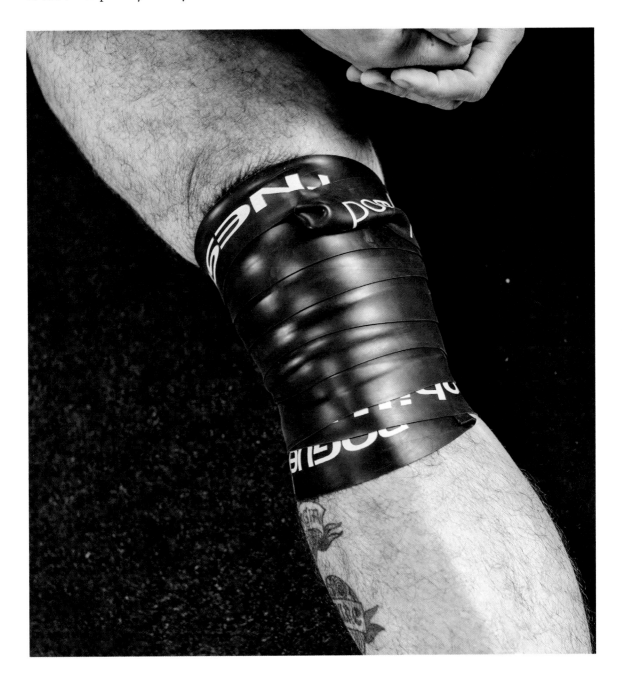

VooDoo Floss Band compression sample 1: tweaky knee

This sequence is an example of how you would use VooDoo Floss Band compression if you were experiencing the all-too-common runner's knee type of inflammation, with pain below your kneecap. Start below your knee and wrap toward your heart, using a half-inch overlap and 75 percent stretch tension, as mentioned above. Tie off the wrap near the top and then floss the tissues by alternatively pointing and flexing your foot for two minutes.

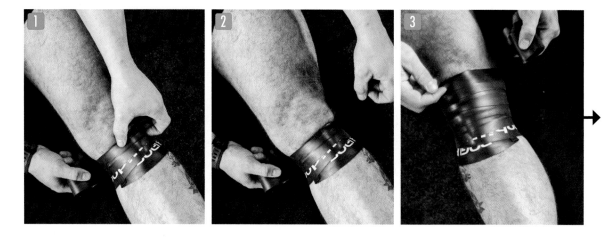

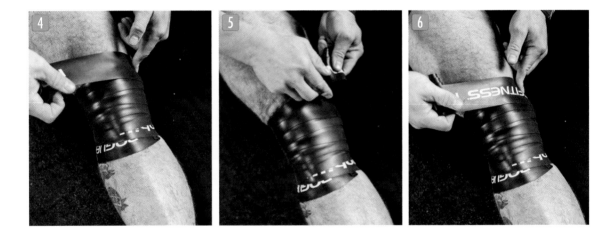

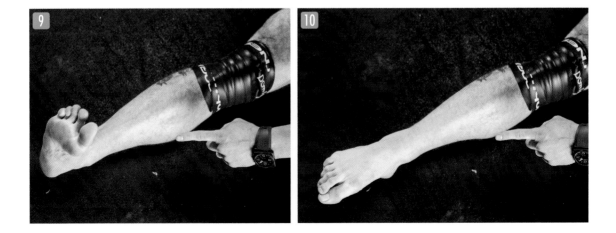

VooDoo Floss Band compression sample 2: iliotibial band pain

Here's an example of how you would use VooDoo Floss Band compression for an annoying pain on the outside of your knee or above your kneecap. After wrapping, start flossing the joint, hamstrings, and quads by executing squats. Use a support if it helps you get into a good, deep position.

VooDoo Floss Band compression sample 3: hamstring pain

For one of those nasty, chronic hamstring tears, wrap center-mass over the hotspot—the middle of the hamstring.

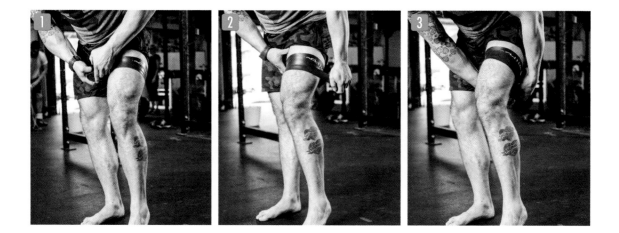

VooDoo Floss Band compression sample 4: Achilles tendon area

After you wrap your ankle as shown in the photos, floss the tissues of the ankle by flexing and extending your foot. You'll feel the band riffle through those sliding surface tissues.

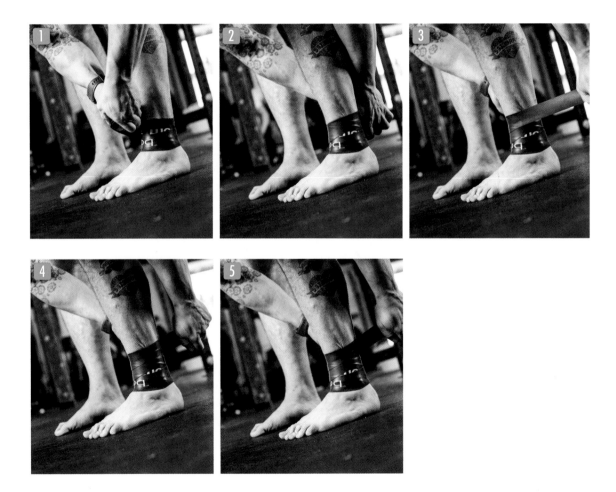

CHAPTER 14
STANDARD #11: HYDRATION

Q: **Are you hydrated?**

Every day, you need to aggressively attend to your body's hydration level. Achieving this standard means that you're drinking at least 2 to 3 liters per day. When you're not drinking your water with food, it should be spiked with electrolytes to facilitate absorption.

KEY MOTIVATION

A hard-training athlete wants to hydrate for several reasons. Failing this standard could cost you as much as 11 percent of your max VO_2—the indicator of how much oxygen your body can process for the sustained output of running power— as well as properly functioning joints and sliding surfaces between the layers of tissue that are getting scorched in your hard workouts. That's just the beginning. However, let's underscore those two items. By simply drinking enough of the right fluids:

- You will not be leaving on the table top-end endurance, *and*
- Your all-important running muscles and connective tissues will be not be parched like tinder for a campfire.

BRIEFING

As a runner, you can't afford the costs of being dehydrated. When your total body water volume is running low, there's less blood available for circulation. When there's less blood available for circulation, your body's delivery of oxygen and nutrients to your tissues is compromised. Less oxygen to your working muscles means less performance.

Water is key to your body's thermoregulation system. The average human loses nearly 3 liters of water a day to breathing, perspiration, and peeing. About 3 cups of that water is lost through—no kidding—the bottoms of the feet. Add running to the equation, and those numbers go up.

Let's talk about your tissues. You were born with these super-amazing tissues that work together to propel you over long distances in your running. There's a lot you can do to take care of them, mend them, and enhance them, and it all starts with hydration. It's not just the water in the individual cells that provides the aqueous environment for your mitochondria to produce energy; it's also the interstitial fluid between cells and all the various balances and counterbalances of electrolytes.

I talk a lot about the value of maintaining good sliding surfaces, particularly around your joints. Specifically, I'm talking about how the various tissues—skin, nerves, muscles, and connective tissues—operate. Do your nerves slide through your muscles? Does your skin slide over your bones? How do interrelated tissues slide and glide with one another? Dehydration is one of the factors that can glue these things together, limiting your range of motion in a key area like your ankle.

Let's talk about your joints and the cartilage between your joints. When cartilage is properly hydrated, the joints glide. Dehydrated cartilage? The joints tend to grind. If you want to rid yourself of rheumatoid pain, you know what's a good place to start? Drinking water and moving around.

When it comes to your body and your performance, water is a smart bomb. It dissolves. It circulates. It removes.

Hydration for an endurance athlete isn't just about diminishing the effects of a hot day. It has everything to do with how you train and how you digest that training.

That's right: When it comes to your body and your performance, water is a smart bomb. It dissolves. It circulates. It removes. It's the solvent in your body, just as water is the solvent in seawater. Enzymatic reactions take place in your body's aqueous environment, and water is the base of your body's capacity to transport antibodies, protein, nutrients, hormones, and all-powerful oxygen through the blood and lymphatic systems.

A 1996 review published in the *Biochemistry Journal*[17] details the deterioration that occurs in a dehydrated state. Muscle cells starved of water fail to properly metabolize proteins and other nutrients and can't properly rebuild themselves. Electrolyte balance is thrown out of whack, and the electrochemical reactions that govern the movement of amino acids across cells slow down. Chronic dehydration robs you of energy and muscle.

If the environment in your body is like a California drought, rationing is put into place. Your brain and body are constantly performing various regulatory mechanisms, and a form of water irrigation is conducted based on availability and priority. If your body is operating at a deficient level of hydration and/or electrolyte levels, the brain robs Peter to pay Paul, so to speak. For example, if there's rationing going on, the creation of new bone marrow will get the available water, and joint cartilage will lose out. The same sorts of things happen when electrolytes are running low.

[17] "The role of cellular hydration in the regulation of cell function," *Biochemistry Journal* 313 (1996), 697-710.

Then there's the subject of sheer performance loss. A 2 percent drop in your optimal body water level can enable max VO_2 power losses of up to 11 percent. This is because, in a hypo-hydrated state, your blood gets more viscous and is not delivering as much oxygen. Also, when your total body water volume is low, there's going to be less water available for muscle contractions as your thermoregulation system works harder to keep your body temperature in check. In other words, more blood goes to your skin and less to your muscle.

Attending to your hydration falls under the No Days Off policy. As a baseline, I recommend that you take in a bare minimum of 2 to 3 liters per day. If you're not drinking this amount of water, ideally most or all of it enhanced with electrolytes, you're failing one of the easiest and most important standards.

Take in a bare minimum of 2 to 3 liters of water per day, ideally most or all of it enhanced with electrolytes.

TAKING HYDRATION WITH A GRAIN OF SALT

Here's a big mistake that athletes trying to hydrate inadvertently make, says Stacy Sims, PhD, an exercise physiologist and specialist in hydration who started the company Osmo. Hour after hour, they keep filling up their aluminum wide-mouth water bottles at the drinking fountain. Two weird things happen: Their trips to the bathroom go through the roof, and they still feel thirsty.

Dr. Sims says the thirst is evidence that the body is not absorbing the water. Even if your pee is clear, you may be suffering from hypo-hydration. The antidote, Dr. Sims says, is a pinch of salt. Mix it in after you fill up your bottle, and your body's digestion system will be better able to absorb the water into your tissues.

The protocol is different at meals. Salt your food ("with simple ol' iodized salt," Dr. Sims says), chase it with pure water, and you're good to go. Eat a lot of watery fruits and vegetables, too. But when you're guzzling water without food, add a pinch of salt.

ADDING FLAVOR

All you really need to ensure that the water sitting in a bottle on your desk doesn't pass through you unabsorbed is a pinch of iodized salt. A $1.50 investment gets you about 26 ounces of Morton's Salt, which is going to last you a long, long time in your quest for hydration.

If you want more flavor and/or convenience, here are a few options to check out. Studies have indicated that when there's more flavor involved, you're likely to drink more fluid (for more on this, see T.J.'s Runner to Runner comments on the next page). This is a theory that you can test out for yourself.

- **Nuun hydration tablets:** Nuun was the first antidote to the sugary world of off-the-shelf sports drinks. Today, these hydration tablets are stocked at a lot of running shoe stores and come in tons of good flavors. Look for the U Natural or All Day Hydration tabs.
- **Nutriforce Sports Balanced Hydration powder:** (*Disclaimer:* I helped with the formula on this one.) In addition to a slate of electrolytes, this powder includes Sustamine, a dipeptide that combines certain amino acids to optimize absorption.
- **Camelbak Elixir tablets:** These were designed for use in the company's hydration backpacks, but you can toss one into a 24-ounce bottle of water and you're good to go.
- **Osmo Nutrition:** This is Dr. Stacy Sims' company, and she's calibrated some of the products to address the different hydration/absorption needs between men and women.

Runner to Runner

In 1998, I had a conversation with an exercise scientist who worked at the Gatorade Sports Science Institute in Barrington, Illinois. He was giving me a tour of one of the labs, a room filled with exercise bikes in which the temperature and humidity could be set to specific numbers. One of the things he told me made perfect sense: Subjects put on the bikes for long periods, riding in a hot room, drank more fluid if the drinks they could reach for contained flavor. He also said that if a subject had a range of flavors to choose from, the athlete seemed to drink even more fluid.

In other words, if you're running 100 miles, you're more apt to stick with a hydration plan if you have more than one flavor to choose from. This is obviously going to vary from individual to individual, but it makes sense. In fact, as the scientist was telling me this, I remembered racing in the Wildflower half-Ironman triathlon on a really hot day. The aid stations had water and lemon-lime Gatorade. Halfway through, I was so sick of the taste of lemon-lime that I couldn't drink any more. That's about as anecdotal as it gets, and nowadays in such a race I would pack my own drink tabs and make my own electrolyte drinks without sugar. But those tabs would probably be a mix of flavors—especially for a race that lasts hours and hours.

—TJM

are you hydrated or not?

If clear urine isn't a surefire signal that you're hydrated, how do you know? For about $12, you can buy 100 urine test strips, like the Rapid Response Urine Dipstick (RRUD), and check to see if you're hydrated well enough. You'll get an amazing amount of information from one dipstick, but the number you want to look at for optimal hydration is the Specific Gravity (SG) marker. Dr. Stacy Sims provides this information on how to read the SG marker and know where you stand:

- Normal hydrated status is 1.005 to 1.015.
- When you approach 1.020, you're slipping. You are about 1 percent down from an optimal total body water volume.
- 1.025? That's even worse. Drink up.

The RRUD strips offer even more objective data for assessing how well you are recovering from your workouts, which can help you avoid the dreaded state of overtraining. Dr. Sims explains the hard information you can exact from one test strip:

- **Leukocytes (LEU):** No change in color indicates that no leukocytes are present. If positive, the reagent will turn purple—the severity of the leukocyte presence will be indicated by the darkness of the purple. If you put in a really hard day of training and the next day the LEU test shows some purple, it would be prudent to back off for at least a day. Sleep, hydrate, increase immune-boosting vitamins and minerals, and keep track of your heart rate and leukocytes.
- **Protein (PRO):** Yellow is normal. Any green in the reagent is a positive marker for protein. In the hours after a workout, it's normal to see some green. But if you wake up the next day and the PRO reagent is still showing green, you haven't fully recovered—a sign that it would be smart for you to make it an easy day of training or take the whole day off.

CHAPTER 15
STANDARD #12:
JUMPING AND LANDING

Q: Can you jump and land with good mechanics?

The mastery of jumping and landing with good mechanics is central to the mastery of good running mechanics. This standard drills deep into the essence of the jumping and landing that running involves.

This is a two-part test: To achieve the standard, you need to be able to jump and land on a box with good mechanics. Second, you must demonstrate the ability to perform 30 single-leg jump-rope hops with your left foot and 30 single-leg hops with your right foot.

KEY MOTIVATION

If you think of running as a virtually endless series of jumps and landings, then it's clear that having a detailed picture of how you jump and how you land is critical for reducing negative forces on your joints and tissues.

recommended mobility exercises for jumping and landing

The simplest, and likely the best, way to improve your jumping and landing mechanics is to jump rope, both double-legged and single-legged. Really tune into how your feet are landing and the path through which your knees are moving. Also try these exercises:

- Double-Ball Ankle Smash & Strip (page 216)
- Plantar Mobilizations (page 217)
- Dorsiflexion Work (page 218)
- Plantar Flexion Overdrive (page 219)
- Adductor Smash (page 222)

BRIEFING

In your journey toward optimal running and optimal running movement, you are probably getting the big picture of all this: that Band-Aids won't suffice. If you're suffering the consequences of a poor set of ingrained mechanics, crappy motor control patterns, and joint positions that encourage wear-and-tear, there is no single, magical answer. Minimalist shoes are not a magical answer. Wearing strips of fashionable athletic tape to get you through a race is not a magical answer. That tape really is a Band-Aid—one that doesn't deter the consequences of your actions.

Rather, to unleash the runner you were born to be, you may have to do a top-to-bottom overhaul of how you move and think about movement.

Fascia and yoga expert Jill Miller likes to talk about one of the dramatic differences between how runners think about movement and how dancers think about movement. Dancers, she says, practice jumps and landings all the time, hours every day, week in and week out. Each time a ballet dancer launches

To unleash the runner you were born to be, you may have to do a top-to-bottom overhaul of how you move and think about movement.

into a jump, the dancer is thinking hard about every piece of that jump and its landing—every angle, every firing muscle, every shape, and every detail. The dancer works with a teacher to address each and every error and perfect that jump.

Until programs like the Pose Method and CrossFit Endurance came along, runners were rarely taught to drill their awareness into the movement skill of running. The countless jumps and landings that runners perform in a lifetime were left unanalyzed.

With this standard, the idea is to zero in on your jumping and landing mechanics and reset poor mechanics. Rather than let the mechanics unfold through the sheer force of repetition, I want you to pay detailed attention to how you pop off the ground and set a new groove—with good patterns and sound mechanics.

This is an important standard to work on. Yet, like the Ankle Range of Motion standard, it can seem overwhelming at first—especially if you've logged tens of thousands of miles of running. That's a lot of time spent sinking yourself into a habitual sequence of movements.

As daunting as such an overhaul might seem, I want to stress that it's not only worth it, but also entirely doable. One tip for making these changes is to understand how a swimming coach like Terry Laughlin, the mastermind behind the Total Immersion program, likes to frame learning how to swim. First, he notes the complexity, saying, "Swimming is the Rubik's Cube of movement skill—highly complex with many interdependent parts." But then he goes on to explain that learning a highly complex activity like swimming is a gift that keeps on giving.

If you attend one of Laughlin's seminars, he is not going to have you jump in the pool, watch you swim, and then start trying to bend your working stroke into something else. Rather, he works with swimmers from a blank slate, essentially building a brand-new stroke from the ground up.

This is similar to how I want you to address this standard of learning how to jump and land correctly. Although jumping and landing might stir up images of that pickup basketball game you avoid because you're sure you'll get hurt, let's talk about what lies at the essence of jumping and landing.

When you jump up in the air and land back on your feet, what you're really doing is performing an unloaded but dynamic squat. As compared with the action of running—a series of pogo stick–like unloaded quarter-squats—the core pattern is the same. Of course, the stress of landing after a max vertical jump is greater, so the opportunity to trash your knees and ankles is higher if your mechanics are faulty. This is why a basketball player who jumps and lands thousands of times with, for example, a knee that caves inward upon landing is whittling away at the patellar tendon into jumper's knee (another way of saying runner's knee) or, worse, an ACL tear.

But if you master jumping and landing with good mechanics, you'll get a feel for good running mechanics. You will put the critical movement pattern involved in your running under the microscope and start to lay a new foundation of quality movement—of moving the way your body is designed to move. And when your body moves the way it's designed to move, it has an incredible capacity to deliver power and use good positions to dissipate the stress of landing.

Effectively transferring the skill of jumping and landing will also pay special dividends in your downhill running or running down steps—situations in which impact stress increases.

If you master jumping and landing with good mechanics, you will put the critical movement pattern involved in running under the microscope and start to lay a new foundation of quality movement—of moving the way your body is designed to move.

POOR JUMPING AND LANDING TECHNIQUE

Let's start by talking about what you don't want and why you don't want it.

Consider sports that involve lateral movements and lots of jumping. If a volleyball or basketball player is jumping and landing with poor mechanics—let's say that his knees collapse inward each time he lands—the stress on his knee complex sets him up to incur one of the more than 250,000 ACL injuries per year in the United States. A good way not to end up a statistic is to jump and land well. Good mechanics are the best medicine.

Some of the faults seen in poor jumping and landing mechanics are essentially the same as the faults seen in poor squatting technique (see page 95). Of course, unlike squatting, where you're stationary, the expression of damage comes much more quickly when you're colliding with the ground with the force of three or more times your body weight. These faults include:

- **Knees forward and shins not vertical.** You lose connection with your posterior chain and hammer your knees.
- **Toes pigeoned inward or fanned outward, duck-like.** You're out of good position and ripping your knees with rotational shear.
- **Unbraced midline and disorganized lumbar spine.** The muscles of your trunk are not engaged, and your pelvis is in a sloppy position. Power from your posterior chain is lost. Your knees get hammered, and so does your lower back.

If you've been getting away with any of these faults and continue to practice them, it's only a matter of time. The bill will show up in the mail, and you will have to pay.

TEST #1: JUMPING ONTO A BOX

Jumping onto a box—whatever size you're comfortable with—is a great exercise for working on your jumping and landing mechanics. Shoot video of your work, or have a friend give you real-time feedback on what you're doing.

Starting position: Load your hips and hamstrings.

Your knees, feet, and back are neutral. Power is coming from your posterior chain.

Land with your knees and feet straight.

Drive your knees outward on landing.

A good landing: knees are driving outward, feet are neutral, and arches are activated.

Fault #1: knees collapsing inward.

Fault #2: open feet. Notice how the arches of the feet and the knees are collapsing.

TEST #2: SINGLE-LEG JUMPS

For this test, you perform 30 single-foot skips with a jump rope, with both your right leg and your left leg, all with good mechanics.

Jumping rope is not only an Autobahn to put to use in reworking your jumping and landing mechanics; it's also a great way to build strength in your feet. It makes a great warm-up for your runs, too. Triple the power!

Use your hips to power your jumps.

Keep a neutral position throughout, from your head through your shoulders through your feet.

Land on your forefoot and allow your heel to lightly kiss the ground before popping up.

Runner to Runner

Working with a jump rope is one of the best ways to prepare your feet and lower legs for replacing heel-striking with a forefoot or mid-foot strike. As Kelly says, it may be the simplest and most straightforward way to strengthen your feet and ankles. My suggestion is to use your jump-rope work as a way to assess your imbalances. One thing I didn't notice when I did jumps with both feet was that my left ankle was considerably weaker than my right ankle. The single-leg jumps were the truth test on this one. I couldn't do a single one-legged jump with my left leg when I started— just trying smarted.

—TJM

Each of the 30 landings for each leg must be with your foot straight and your knee in a neutral position.

FAULT: collapsing arch and valgus knee.

PART 3

You are a system of systems. Knee pain, back pain, and arch pain are not independent issues—they are specific expressions of problems that have multidimensional properties within the body. In being truly Ready to Run, it is essential that you understand and apply this concept.

How do you do this? After you've tested yourself against the 12 standards, you will have a working picture of where your body, your lifestyle, and your habits stand. You will know what your strengths are—a valuable confirmation—and, more importantly, you'll have clear evidence of your weaknesses. This is where the money is—in turning your weaknesses into strengths that will fully prepare you for both the joy and the rigor that running well has to offer. Let's get started.

CHAPTER 16
INTRODUCTION TO MOBILITY WORK

Testing how you fare against the 12 standards will present you with a working snapshot of how Ready to Run you are, but, more importantly, it will help you pinpoint your major weaknesses. These known shortcomings are what I refer to as your goats. In the context of *Ready to Run,* a goat can be any of these four types:

- **A lifestyle issue (such as not standing with neutral feet)**
- **A mobility issue (such as poor hip extension)**
- **A position issue (such as being unable to squat well)**
- **An issue of mechanics (such as poor jumping and landing technique)**

As you've no doubt concluded by now, these different types of goats are interrelated. If you live your life wearing high-heeled shoes (a lifestyle issue), for example, it can have a direct effect on your joint mobility, which can affect your mechanics.

I often see this pattern with runners and other athletes who are struggling with poor performance, injuries, or both.

LIFESTYLE ERROR

(dehydration, wearing overbuilt shoes, sitting too much,
duck-walking)

MOBILITY PROBLEMS

(stiff, unhealthy tissues; range of motion restrictions;
hotspots)

POSITION PROBLEMS

(unable to get into correct squatting positions,
unable to sustain good spinal positions)

MOVEMENT PROBLEMS

(unable to run without arches and knees collapsing inward)

PERFORMANCE PROBLEMS

(pain, injury, power loss)

By keeping your focus on the 12 standards, you are addressing a set of exceptionally important targets that will place you on a trajectory toward being able to run well and enjoy an athletic life free from the sorts of chronic injuries that drive many runners toward psychosis.

So what's next? You have tested your 12 standards. You passed certain standards and didn't pass others.

First of all, I want you to consider any test that you failed reason to celebrate. Not wearing compression socks? Sweet, that's an easy one. Your ankle range of motion sucks? Fantastic. The answer isn't at easy as buying a new pair of socks, but it's an opportunity nonetheless.

Celebrate the opportunity. It is performance just lying there waiting for you to grab it. With each goat on your list, you have a specific and worthy goal shimmering on the horizon, waiting for you to chase it. It may take time and persistence, because enhancing your mobility and improving your mechanics are not overnight affairs, but by making progress toward these targets, you will earn better performance and increased durability.

So how do you work toward a perfect *Ready to Run* score?

First, look at your report card and circle the standards that you're falling short on.

Falling short on any of the standards is an opportunity to celebrate—it is performance just lying there waiting for you to grab it.

LIFESTYLE/ADAPTATION STANDARDS

- Neutral feet
- Flat shoes
- Warming up and cooling down
- Compression
- Hydration

MOBILITY/MOTOR CONTROL STANDARDS

- Supple thoracic spine
- Squatting technique
- Hip flexion
- Hip extension
- Ankle range of motion
- No hotspots
- Jumping and landing

Now that you've identified your goats, you're ready to jump into action. With the lifestyle/adaptation standards, you can change things like hydrating properly, warming up and cooling down, and wearing compression socks *today*. If you've been wearing shoes with built-up heels, you will need to patiently work your way toward wearing flat shoes (use the 10 percent plan described on page 76). Making neutral feet a habit will also take time, but it too is something toward which you can make big strides in a matter of hours.

A great thing about diving into correcting lifestyle/adaptation errors is that it will support your work on improving on your mobility/motor control shortfalls. The direct work of improving on each of the mobility and motor control standards is the focus of the rest of this book.

IMPROVING YOUR MOBILITY: A STRATEGIC APPROACH

When it comes to performing maintenance, there is no one-size-fits-all program for runners. As you've probably gleaned by now, the aches and pains that can interfere with running well can be created by myriad forces, from an inability to get into good positions to specific tissue problems, like an inflamed heel. What you need is a system that you can use to attack your particular issues—a system that prioritizes fixing the underlying problems but also addresses the nagging symptoms.

Even better, this systematized approach should be a concrete, everyday discipline (like brushing and flossing your teeth) so that you can *prevent* problems altogether, well before pain and injuries surface.

Whether you're a distance runner, a sprinter, or a soccer player or you're training for the CrossFit Games, pursuing and achieving the 12 *Ready to Run* standards offers you the benefit of preventing injuries that you might otherwise be destined for. Rather than waiting for a tendon strain or an inflamed knee to crop up in order to communicate to you that you are doing something wrong, create an injury prevention discipline by spending 10 to 20 minutes a day working to make your weaknesses strengths and by using good mechanics not just when you're training, but throughout your day. This discipline, or system, is far more productive than the whack-a-mole game that many athletes get into, where they desperately try to stamp out symptoms rather than deal with the underlying causes.

For your mission to achieve the 12 standards, the mobility exercises outlined in Chapter 17 are surgical instruments designed to instigate change. Your test results will show you where you're currently deficient. Again, these are your goats. The mobilizations are designed to unglue these areas of restriction and compromised tissue.

I want to emphasize that daily attention to mobility work is just one aspect of the *Ready to Run* construct. It's one part of a three-part approach:

1. **Lifestyle.** Make sure that your lifestyle choices are in order. Proper hydration, flat shoes, compression socks, neutral feet at all times—remember to attend to these simple yet powerful disciplines.
2. **Mobility.** Make sure that you are working toward or maintaining the mobility standards, like hip extension and ankle range of motion.
3. **Mechanics.** Make sure that you are jumping, landing, and squatting correctly. With lifestyle and mobility humming along well, you have the ability to get into and practice good positions and good mechanics. From here, you can further refine your mastery of running by taking on the Pose Method or a similar running-form technique.

Before you begin your work on developing optimal mobility for running, I want to talk you through the essential principles for getting the most out of these 10 minutes a day.

MOBILITY WORK: GUIDING PRINCIPLES

As you commit yourself to achieving the 12 standards, use the following principles to guide your work.

- **AT LEAST 10 MINUTES A DAY**

  I advise my athletes to strive for 20 minutes or more per day of mobility work, but I also know that a typical day in the modern world can run amok. So what I'm asking of you is a blood commitment to at least 10 minutes a day, every day. You can make incredible progress toward achieving the mobility standards with a mere 10 minutes per day. It's only 10 minutes, but it needs to be 10 minutes charged with purpose. Pick a target area for the day, be it your feet, your hamstrings, or your glutes, and pepper that area with mobility work.

  No matter what, get that 10 minutes in every day. But I also want you to take those spare moments you have during the day to squeeze in a little extra Couch Stretch time (see page 114), or mobility work on your feet, or time spent in a squat position. I want you to work toward netting a full 20 minutes a day of quality mobility and tissue work. But first and foremost, get in your 10 minutes.

- **TWO MINUTES OR MORE**

  Spend two minutes of dedicated work on each mobilization. Two minutes is the minimum amount of time you need to effect real change in your tissue. If your mobilization of the day is the Couch Stretch, for example, then perform the Couch Stretch for two minutes on the right side and then two minutes on the left side. You'll notice a change. Just two minutes does wonders. But it has to be a *focused* two minutes. If you see people at the gym haphazardly lazing back onto foam rollers while they read emails on their phones, they are not mobilizing. You're much better off spending two targeted minutes working intently with a specific mobilization than rolling around without focus for 20 minutes.

To make your daily mobility time count, pick one or two mobilizations and go in with total purpose. To effect real change, you need to work smartly and deeply, searching for knots and particularly tight areas. Two minutes for each mobilization can be very effective, but you must work with focus and concentration.

- **WORK UPSTREAM AND DOWNSTREAM**
  To make real improvements on your goats, work upstream and downstream of the problem. In other words, if a certain area, joint, or muscle, be it your ankle, knee, hamstring, hip, or lower back, is a source of injury or is preventing you from attaining a standard, then, in addition to using VooDoo Floss Band compression (see page 150) on the area or taking a lacrosse ball to the site of pain or restriction, you have to develop some slack around the problem. Sure, you want to work directly on the hotspot or restricted area, but you also want to work above and below the problem. Why? Because it helps you create slack around the joint or tissue hotspot.

  If you have terrible ankle range of motion, for example, then dedicate some of your mobility time to working below the problem area (your arches, your toes, and the tops of your feet) and above the problem area (your calf muscles, your knees, and even your upper legs and hips).

- **IF IT FEELS SKETCHY, IT IS SKETCHY**

  If you're mobilizing and really pushing it, you may get a pain signal that is less about the stress being placed on the muscle tissue and more about hitting a nerve in a bad way. So here's the rule: If it feels sketchy, it is sketchy. Back off and go about the mobilization in a different way.

  For example, behind the knee is a neuromuscular bundle that you might come in contact with while you're doing leg flexion work, working a lacrosse ball like you might use a nutcracker. Spots like these sometimes send up spots of weird, nervy pain. This is the time to back off. While you want to push deep and peel back layers of discomfort with your mobility work, if the signal coming from your body says, "This is wrong," then it is wrong.

- **BE CREATIVE**

  The mobility exercises that I outline in this book are starting points. Don't be contained to the mobilizations. As you'll note in many of the descriptions, I want you to poke around and seek out hidden areas that are especially trashed. Try different tools and techniques to sort things out. Have fun with it, and always work with intent.

  For example, say your plan is to spend your 10 minutes on your calves. You've been doing some fast running on the track or shuttle running in a CrossFit workout, and your gastrocs are smoked. So one of your mobilizations for the day is to perform a Calf Smash with a lacrosse ball. You start by placing the ball in the belly of your calf and smashing it into the hotspot for two minutes. But then you start hunting, playing around with looping a stretch band around your foot, still working with the ball smashed to the ground under your calf. You then riffle through some of the techniques laid out in the following section, like contract-relax and pressure wave. Let your intuition lead you into new techniques and combinations of techniques.

- **USE GOOD POSITIONS**

  Pay attention to your posture and positions when you work on mobilizations. Keep a braced neutral spine (see page 65), and don't let your knees collapse inward. As I stress throughout this book, you must follow this principle throughout your day, not just during your workouts. You're an athlete 24 hours a day. If you're able to spend less time sitting at the office, for example, that's less time spent in a bad position that yields tissue problems, meaning that you'll be able to cut back on the amount of mobilizing you might be doing to counter those sitting-related problems. Tune into your mechanics and try to be in a good position all the time. Your running will reap powerful benefits.

- **NO DAYS OFF**

  There's a bad habit that some runners have. I've brought it up before, but it's worth mentioning again here because it's so crucial to establishing an effective maintenance program. It's the bad habit of finishing a workout and leaving your identity as an athlete behind until the next time you train. This habit is exhibited in the runner who polishes off a 6-mile morning run and then heads to the office to spend the rest of the day slightly slumped in a chair, or walks around with poor mechanics, knees caving in or shoulders slumped forward. It's like working hard to use good form for five sets of deadlifts, then sitting down on the ground to rest between sets and using the crappiest mechanics imaginable to get up.

  The No Days Off policy is a mindset, and it starts with the understanding that your muscles mold around the positions you use most. If you spend a good part of your day sitting in a chair, then your muscles and joints are going to sway toward that flexed position. The time you clock in bad positions throughout the day tends to leak into the positions and mechanics you favor while running.

The antidote is make it a habit to constantly scan the positions you're using. The more you use good positions and move with good mechanics, the more your running will benefit. Every movement and position you use counts, whether you're 18, 25, 43, or 75.

Think of it this way: Every few years, you check your mailbox and there it is: a new credit card to replace your old one. You open the envelope and take out the new card. Before you peel off the sticker, you grab your phone and make the activation call. After that, you have one more job: to extract the old credit card from your wallet and commit to the act of destruction.

It's not easy—you bend that credit card in half once, and then repeat by bending it the other way, back and forth and back and forth. Amazing how resilient it is, isn't it? Credit cards are built to take abuse.

And so are you. If you think of each performance of a flawed gait cycle of running like a back-and-forth bend of a credit card, your tissues can handle a tremendous number of reps. One day, though, as surprising as it might be, a slight tear occurs in your tissues, just as a slight crack appears in the credit card.

There are no days off when it comes to maintenance. Even on the busiest of days, you can commit to finding 10 minutes for mobility work.

You keep going because you can. But one day, the tissue gives. As the credit card ultimately breaks in half, a hole is worn into your knee, or a disc gives out.

This is an essential metaphor to support the No Days Off policy. While taking an occasional day off from training is prudent and built into most running programs, there are no days off when it comes to maintenance. Even on the busiest of days, you can commit to finding 10 minutes for mobility work.

Why? Because each minute you invest in movement and mobility work helps prevent and reduce the minute wreckage that occurs with each step of running. That damage isn't a big deal on its own, but multiply it by a million, and you've just pushed that old credit card into an industrial shredder.

Commit to never taking a day off from your maintenance work. To do so, build maintenance work into your daily routine.

Many of the mobilizations presented in this book require little tweaking to be made a part of the regular flow of your day. Use the Couch Stretch (see page 114) while you're watching TV, for example. Or set a timer to go off every hour, reminding you to get out of your chair and walk around, sip some water, and maybe perform a good calf mob or drop into a deep one-minute squat.

TECHNIQUES

At my mobility clinics, I want the participants to leave with a set of tools that enable them to cover all the necessary groundwork in the pursuit of optimal mobility. Like a craftsman has specific techniques for specific jobs, or a golfer needs woods, irons, and a putter, athletes and coaches need a set of mobilization techniques that cover the gamut of their needs. You need a different technique for improving the position of your hip joint than you do for a patch of sticky sliding surfaces in the arch of your foot, for example.

The following are the core techniques that I teach in my mobility system. Many of them can be used in combination, like a one-two punch. For example, if you want to address a hotspot deep in your hamstring, it is a good time to use both a pressure wave and a contract-relax move, one after the other. This sort of multifaceted attack will help you achieve the best results with a minimal investment of time. The tools you'll use to execute these techniques are covered in the section "Your Mobility Toolbox," beginning on page 196.

smash

contract-relax

- **SMASH**

  The smash is a compression-based plumb-bob technique. In other words, it enables you to get a look into what's going on in the depths of your tissues. To perform a basic smash, place a ball or roller on the area you wish to work, take a breath, let it out, and allow your muscles to relax around the mobility tool. As you'll see, many of the mobilization techniques start off with a smash.

- **CONTRACT-RELAX**

  You've probably heard of contract-relax: It's an established neuromuscular technique that does wonders to improve range of motion. Here's an example of how you might use contract-relax: If you hit a hotspot with the basic smash, it's natural for your body to respond by tensing that muscle. You counter by contracting the muscle with an inhale and then relaxing the muscle with an exhale, allowing the ball or roller to sink deeper into the tissue. Repeat this process several times. The contract-relax technique enables mechanisms that will relax away this tension and permit you to go deeper into the problem area, interacting with trigger points and generating relief. You can also use it when you're working on muscle tissues in end-range positions by tensing the muscle for a few seconds, then relaxing the muscle for a few seconds, then deepening the position. Repeat this process several times.

  Contract-relax is a good technique for improving sliding surface function as well. When you're using a ball on a specific spot—say, your heel cord—to improve the sliding surfaces within the tissue, press deep with the ball, then contract your foot into a flexed position for a few seconds. Then relax your foot, press the ball deeper, and repeat.

- **PRESSURE WAVE**

  The pressure wave is for pinpointed work and is highly effective for deep-tissue needs, like a deep knot in your hip. To do it, place a ball or roller on the spot you intend to work, then use your body weight to sink the ball deep into the tissue. Again, you're using a basic smash. Then slowly move the tissue back and forth across the ball or roller, creating a pressure wave. This move is akin to a Rolfer sinking an elbow into your hip and then moving it back and forth across the knot.

pressure wave

- **STRIPPING**

  Stripping is simply using a ball or roller along the grain of muscle tissue to comb through the various fascias and fibers. The key with this maneuver is to work very slowly. If you bust out a roller, lie on it, and then move at the speed of a pinball, you're going to accomplish absolutely nothing of value.

  Say you decide to strip your quads. Start off with a smash to get good and deep into the tissue, and then ever so slowly roll through the muscle from above your knee to your hip bone. It should feel like shoveling through a layer of wet snow.

stripping

- **SMASH AND FLOSS**

  Let's revisit sliding surfaces briefly. Your body is a vast network of interconnected tissues. In the physical therapy world, the term "regional interdependencies" is often used to describe how we need to consider a spectrum of muscles and tissues within and surrounding a hotspot when we go about treating a patient. When I talk about restoring sliding surfaces, I'm talking about dealing with sticky, matted-down tissues that ultimately impair your range of motion. For example, let's say that your standards tests showed that you have extremely poor range of motion in

smash and floss

your ankles. Restoring the sliding surfaces is going to be a key component of opening up those ankles.

Smash and floss is a vital technique for restoring the natural glide that should exist between layers of skin, muscle, nerves, and fascias that can get all bundled up. The basic smash and floss goes like this: You use the smash technique to position a ball or roller deep in the tissue. In the ankle example, imagine you're placing the ball in the muscle of your lower calf. Then you begin the flossing by moving your foot and ankle through as much range of motion as you can muster, back and forth. This movement flosses the ball through the tissues and helps you restore slide and glide.

global shear

- ## GLOBAL SHEAR
  So far I've been talking a lot about moves that zero in on a specific location. Global shear is designed to rake through large muscles or a range of muscles all at once. For example, say you want to work on your thoracic spine mobility. You can do some great detail work with a ball, but it might be helpful to start by using a roller to shear up and down your back to create some general release and warm up the tissue for the deeper work to come.

flexion gapping

- ## FLEXION GAPPING
  Flexion gapping is a specific joint-capsule technique to address a tight, gummed-up knee. You simply put a ball or rolled-up towel behind your knee and then pull your leg into full flexion. The gap created by the ball or towel creates a force that can help you develop full range of motion.

tack and twist

- ## TACK AND TWIST
  Tack and twist is another great move for restoring sliding surface function. You smash a ball—preferably a softer ball that has some grippiness to it—into the tissue to tack

things down and then give the ball a twist. This technique helps you brush through stiff tissue as well as move blood into areas where circulation is relatively weak, like the heel cord.

- **BANDED FLOSSING**
Flossing basically means moving a limb back and forth or side to side. For the banded flossing technique, you loop a heavy-duty band around a joint or muscle—say, around your high hamstring—and then begin moving your leg through a squat or lunge. Adding banded flossing to a mobilization enables you to gain additional range of motion, in this case by helping you reset your hip capsule.

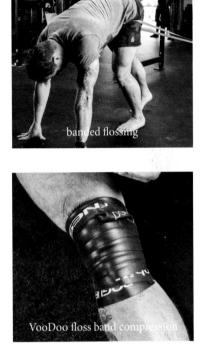

banded flossing

VooDoo floss band compression

- **VOODOO FLOSS BAND COMPRESSION**
I covered VooDoo Floss Band compression in the No Hotspots standard (see page 150), but it's so valuable for athletes that I want to review it here as well. VooDoo Floss Band compression is a pathway to create a high-powered shearing effect on a tissue hotspot, chunk of scar tissue, or compromised joint. Wrapping a band around the area returns sliding surface function to the area, and, after you take off the band, blood flows into those joints and tissues. Muscle contraction improves, joint mobility improves, and sliding surfaces are refreshed. Voodoo Compressing a swollen joint forces the swelling back into the lymphatic system, where it can drain from the body.

To do VooDoo Floss Band compression, you use a compression band—or you can use a deflated bike tire cut in two. Start below the target area and wrap toward your heart, with a half-inch overlap of each loop and about 50 percent stretch in the band. Cover all the skin as you wrap up and over the target area, increasing the tension of the wrap to 75 percent in the target area itself. With the band wrapped around the joint or hotspot, spend time moving your foot or leg throughout its range of motion. This can suck a bit, but embrace it. After a few minutes, unwrap and take some time to recover. Then repeat after a few minutes.

If you are using VooDoo Floss Band compression to help restore sliding surfaces, aim for at least two sessions. If you are using it to counter swelling and inflammation from a more acute injury, then shoot for a minimum of five sessions, with a maximum of 10.

---

don't ice

One of the things that's become crystal clear, both in the clinical research on the topic and in the practice of top professional sports leagues, is that using ice with the intention of healing an injury is counterproductive.

Will ice numb an area and decrease pain? Yes—but at a specific cost. Applying ice to an inflamed area not only numbs the pain, but also shuts off communication between the muscles and nerves. The upshot? The flow of the lymphatic system—the all-powerful system in your body that does the healing—is reversed.

Here's an example of what the scientific literature has to say about the effect of icing:

> "When ice is applied to a body part for a prolonged period, nearby lymphatic vessels begin to dramatically increase their permeability (lymphatic vessels are 'dead-end' tubes which ordinarily help carry excess tissue fluids back into the cardiovascular system). As lymphatic permeability is enhanced, large amounts of fluid begin to pour from the lymphatics 'in the wrong direction' (into the injured area), increasing the amount of local swelling and pressure and potentially contributing to greater pain."[18]

[18] "The Use of Cryotherapy in Sports Injuries," *Sports Medicine* 3 (1986), 398-414.

Gary Reinl of Marc Pro is an expert on the subject of icing and a consultant to a who's-who list of trainers for top professional sports teams. "Icing congests the tissues," Reinl says, and points out that not a single medical textbook or clinical study supports the use of icing to heal injuries.

Using ice or ibuprofen (which Reinl says is even worse than icing) with the intention of preventing inflammation is a mistake. "Why would you want to do that?" he asks. In other words, why would you want to try to take over the regulation of the inflammatory response when the inflammatory response is a necessary stage in healing?

Here's my main point: Without inflammation, healing cannot occur.

What helps the lymphatic system do its job? It's the exact opposite of the first step of the RICE protocol (rest, ice, compression, elevation): movement rather than rest. Movement helps the lymphatic system begin the process of restoring the tissues. The next time you turn your ankle or pick up some inflammation in your knee, instead of reaching for the ice, give VooDoo Floss Band compression and movement of the limb a complete test/retest.

Why has using ice to treat athletic injuries been so common over the last few decades? Reinl believes that it started back in the 1960s on NFL sidelines. Ice was cheap and easy to get, and it stopped the pain. But to this day there is no clinical research supporting the method.

Don't take my word for it: Check it out for yourself. For more information, read Reinl's book, *Iced! The Illusionary Treatment Option* (Amazon Digital Services).

YOUR MOBILITY TOOLBOX

With $10 and a trip to a garage sale or thrift store, you can get a great start on building a world-class mobility gym. Or you can make do with even less. Grab some common items from your garage, kitchen, and closets, and you can start mobilizing within the hour. A wine bottle. A barbell. A section of pipe. A softball. A baseball. A golf ball. A half-deflated soccer ball. A punctured bike tire tube. Any of these household items can be used for mobility work.

As you deepen your practice, there is plenty of useful stuff to buy. Or not. The most important thing is to do the work. A consistent practice is an effective practice. If you blow $200 on rollers, balls, and mobility devices but abandon them in the garage, they're worthless.

With that in mind, the following are the tools that I believe are worth investing in when you're ready to upgrade from the stuff you find around the house.

- **ROLLER**

  Good for: contract-relax, pressure wave, stripping, smash and floss, global shear

  You probably already have a foam roller or have access to a foam roller at the gym—they've become ubiquitous. To be blunt, I think foam rollers are fine for beginners and children, but to effect the kind of change an athlete needs for top performance, you need a tool that can penetrate deeper into your tissues and create more shear. But you do need some type of roller. Opt for something with a little more bite to it, like the Rumble Roller (a roller made with rubber teeth), a pipe, or a barbell.

- ### BATTLESTAR

  Good for: contract-relax, pressure wave, stripping, smash and floss, global shear

  An extreme upgrade to the standard foam roller. I like to equate the Battlestar with what you'd get if you combined a chainsaw, a wolverine, and a steamroller. I designed this tool to execute both the global shearing of a hard foam roller and acute, detailed raking work. (Available at www.roguefitness.com)

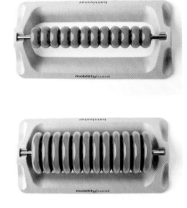

- ### LACROSSE BALLS

  Good for: contract-relax, pressure wave, stripping, smash and floss, flexion gapping

  Lacrosse balls are firm enough that they can sink deep into your tissues. Even if they are all you have, you can do some incredible mobility work. You can pick up a few lacrosse balls at the nearest sporting goods store. Each ball is going to set you back about two bucks.

  A double-lacrosse-ball setup is especially valuable for working on your shins and your thoracic spine. Take two lacrosse balls, grab a roll of athletic tape, loop the tape two or three times around both balls at once, and then wrap the tape around the center between the two balls. You're ready to mobilize.

- ### YOGA TUNE UP THERAPY BALLS

  Good for: contract-relax, pressure wave, stripping, smash and floss, tack and twist

  From fascia and pain relief expert Jill Miller, these balls are about the same size as lacrosse balls, but are softer and have a stickier surface. They give you a different spin on the techniques for which you could also use a lacrosse ball, but

they're especially useful for tacking and twisting tissues, such as those on the top of your foot, and breathing some life into your fascias. A pair, as pictured, comes with a tote bag, so you can use it as you would a double-lacrosse-ball setup. (Available at www.yogatuneup.com)

- **ALPHA BALL**

  Good for: contract-relax, pressure wave, stripping, smash and floss, tack and twist

  Another of Jill Miller's tools, this ball is 3.5 inches in diameter, a bit soft, and a bit sticky, so it's good for hotspot work when you're trying to unglue stuck sliding surface tissue and you may be putting some weight into your skeleton. (Available at www.yogatuneup.com)

- **GEMINI**

  Good for: smash, contract-relax, stripping, smash and floss

  I started off with the double-lacrosse-ball setup for work on the T-spine, where it's ideal for blocking off the facet joints, but this tool provides more detail and grip to get a little more out of targeted trigger point work. (Available at www.roguefitness.com)

- **SOFTBALL**

  Good for: smash, contract-relax, pressure wave, stripping, smash and floss

  Sometimes you need an object larger than a lacrosse ball to get where you need to go with a smash. A softball is to your mobility work what a fat Sharpie marker is to your selection of writing tools. It's especially good for smashing into the large glute muscles.

- **SUPERNOVA**

  Good for: smash, contract-relax, pressure wave, stripping, smash and floss

  An upgrade on the softball, the Supernova was invented to dole out a much higher percentage of grip and shear when working into a deep pocket of tissue, like the hip or hamstring. The teeth of the Supernova are designed to separate the many layers of tissue that you need to penetrate for optimal mobilization. (Available at www.roguefitness.com)

- **SOCCER BALL**

  Good for: smash, contract-relax, global shear

  Rather than explain this, I think it's best that you just try it. You'll instantly get the message. Get your hands on a soccer ball at a garage sale or thrift store, or raid your kid's closet. Let out some of the air, and then sprawl on top of the ball so that it hits you in the gut. Then begin rolling around. At some point, you'll trip over your psoas, the long muscle running through half your body that is responsible for flexing your hip, among other things. In athletes—especially athletes who run a lot—the psoas gets incredibly tight, setting off a wide range of mobility troubles. Performing the smash with a deflated soccer ball is your new secret weapon toward meeting the Hip Flexion, Hip Extension, and Efficient Squatting Technique standards.

- **COREGEOUS BALL**

  Good for: smash, contract-relax, global shear

  This is a high-end upgrade on a half-deflated soccer ball. Jill Miller's inflatable 9-inch ball has the added value of being a little bit sticky, so you can tack the ball into a spot and work on the dreaded psoas. (Available at www.yogatuneup.com)

- ## Rogue Monster Band

  Good for: contract-relax, banded flossing

  This robust rubber band is especially valuable when your mobility work of the day is targeting your hamstrings and glutes. (Available at www.roguefitness.com)

- ## VooDoo Floss Band

  Good for: VooDoo Floss Band compression

  The VooDoo Floss band is engineered for therapeutic compression on hotspots and swollen joints, as detailed in the No Hotspots standard. A household alternative is to splice a bike tire tube lengthwise. (Available at www. roguefitness.com)

- ## Ab mat

  An ab mat is a good all-around tool to have in your mobility toolkit. You'll use it for the Couch Stretch (see page 114), but it's always good to have on hand if you require some extra cushion or support for your lower lumbar spine. (Available at www.roguefitness.com)

going deep

At the heart of *Ready to Run* is a single, guiding mission for athletes: You have to go deep. If you wait until something hurts, you're acting way too late.

Typically, runners and other athletes do their sport until one day—wham—they wake up to discover that their knee hurts, or their Achilles tendon is sore, or they have a hamstring tear.

At this point, the athlete swoops into action, treating the symptoms with ice, ibuprofen, and the like, waiting for the pain to go away and then springing back into action.

This is the classic treat-the-symptoms approach. In the *Ready to Run* system, treating symptoms is part of the game plan, sure (VooDoo Floss Band compression is an important action to take when you have swelling and pain in a joint or tissue—see page 150), but it's secondary to treating the root cause. The root cause can always be found in either your ability to get into good positions (your mobility, particularly in regard to your ankles, knees, and hips) or your motor control patterns (your mechanics, such as the patterns you habitually use when you jump and land).

By periodically testing yourself on the 12 standards, you can usually stop an injury in its tracks long before it is expressed. If you can't squat well or you don't have normal, healthy hip flexion or extension, that's an alert that an injury is waiting to get a hold of you someday. It's also a sign that you're leaking away energy and power that could be better used toward performance.

Some people might argue that because the act of running itself uses a relatively limited range of motion, developing the range of motion and capacity to get into good positions is excessive. The logic goes that to be a runner, you really don't need to get into a full squat, and you don't really need the amount of ankle range of motion and hip function called for in the *Ready to Run* standards.

But for me, it's about having a buffer. When you need to jump in the car and do a solid piece of driving to take care of an errand or make a meeting, isn't it nice to have a full tank of gas? Sure, you could probably make it there and back on a quarter tank, but isn't the ideal situation the one in which you know you've got it covered?

The same philosophy applies to the mobility standards. By achieving each standard, you can rest assured that your body is capable of getting into good positions and using good movement patterns. The tank is full.

CHAPTER 17
MOBILIZATIONS

You've tested yourself across the 12 standards, and you now have a good idea of what weaknesses (I call them goats) stand between you and being Ready to Run. The mobility exercises in this chapter will help you improve on your goats from two directions:

1. They will help you figure out the source of a weakness and work through that specific tissue restriction.
2. They will help you create slack around the problem by working upstream and downstream of the weak area.

These two attacks will help you improve your mobility and eventually turn a goat into a strength.

THE MOBILIZATION WORKOUT

When it's time to perform your mobility work for the day, how do you proceed? You may know which *Ready to Run* standards you need to make progress on, and you may also have a hotspot here or there. So what's the protocol?

1. **Work on hotspots first.** Did you feel a twinge in your foot or your Achilles near the end of a run or MetCon? Is you knee a bit stiff and tweaky? The first thing you want to address in your mobility session is any sign of a hotspot or signal that there may be a hotspot in your future. For example, let's say you felt pain creeping around the inside of your knee during a run. This pain would be the first thing you would attend to in your mobility session. VooDoo Floss Band compression followed by an upstream and a downstream mobilization would be a good plan for a minor tweaky feeling or ache. If it's a significant hotspot, dedicate at least 10 minutes to working on the problem area and upstream and downstream of the problem.

2. **Work on a goat.** From your test results, pick a goat to work on. Say you are short of the Ankle Range of Motion standard, for example. Choose one or two of the lower leg mobilizations and spend at least two minutes per side with each exercise. If you have time, work in an appropriate upper leg mobilization to get in some upstream work.

3. **Do maintenance mobility work.** If you still have some time, cycle through another area, either a second goat or a standard you are already meeting. For example, say you have a supple thoracic spine. That's super—let's keep it that way. Spend two minutes doing some global work on your upper back.

I want you to invest a minimum of 10 minutes per day, every day, year-round, with this template in mind. Ten minutes is solid, but if you can find the extra minutes, put in two mobility sessions per day, or add mobilization time to your warm-up or cool-down, and your improvements will come that much faster.

LOWER LEG

Calf Smash & Pressure Wave

Working on your calves is a gnarly business. Runners know this—these muscles are short, abused, and sensitive as hell. The Calf Smash is a good place to start, and it can be a nice mobilization to throw into your pre-run warm-up. Performing the Calf Smash will likely reveal tight patches and knots that you didn't know you had. When you find those, swoop in with the Pressure Wave.

Want some extra pressure? Use a sandbag or loaded backpack to perform a Weighted Calf Smash.

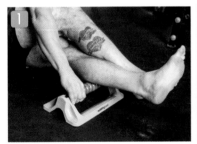

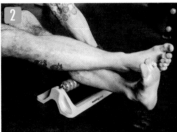

Place your calf on top of the roller of your choice, or a pipe or barbell. Use your other leg to apply some extra pressure and weight.

Relax your muscles, breathe, and sink into the roller to connect with your deepest tissues. Now move into the Pressure Wave, slowly rolling your lower leg from side to side and kneading your way into the tissues.

Contract and relax the tissues by flexing and extending your foot through its full range of motion.

Banded Ankle Mob 1

Using a band is a powerful technique for maintaining the health and position of a joint capsule. It also helps revive sticky sliding surfaces. In fact, the pounding that athletes take from running often results in skin being stuck to the Achilles tendon, which, unsurprisingly, can create problems. If the tissues around your heel cords are beat to hell, take a band and loop one end around a post and the other end around your heel. Move out to create as much tension in the band as you can. Keep your foot flat on the ground throughout this mobilization. Test your ankle range of motion before and after to register any change.

Hook a Rogue Monster Band around your heel.

Keeping your foot flat on the ground, drive your knee forward and out. Do not to let your knee collapse inward.

Oscillate back and forth to restore the sliding tissues around the joint.

Banded Ankle Mob 2

In this variation of the Banded Ankle Mob, you drop your rear knee to the floor, use your hand to push your other knee outward, and work through the entire ankle—working toward those corners in search of tight spots to be dealt with. Test your ankle range of motion before and after this mobilization to see if there's a change in your tissues.

Wrap the band around the front of your ankle, get some good tension in the band, and then drop your opposite knee to the ground.

Use your hand to press your knee outward, keeping your foot flat on the ground.

Bone Saw Calf Smash

The Bone Saw is a potent way to work on your dorsiflexion range of motion and the fascias within your feet and ankles. As your ability increases, work through the positions shown in the photos to the point where you can sit back on your lower leg for optimal pressure. Don't be surprised if you start sweating while you're doing this mobilization—that's your fascias being challenged.

Lower yourself so that the front of your ankle complex is supported by an ab mat or a folded towel.

Cross your opposite ankle on top of the calf you're working on.

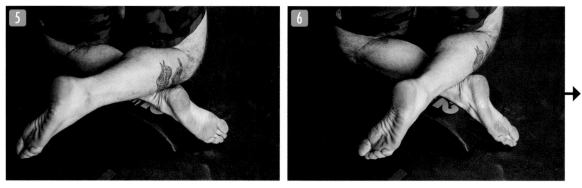

You can also move up and down along the tissues, tacking and flossing those matted sliding surfaces.

Move your hips up and down in a contract-relax fashion.

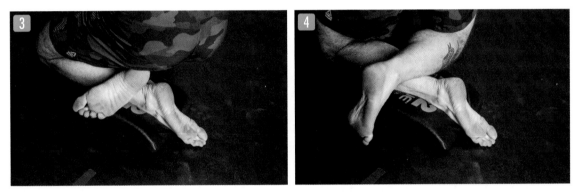

Sit back to apply as much pressure as you can handle without things getting sketchy. This is the smash part.

This is the saw part—in the photo, my right leg is sawing into my left calf.

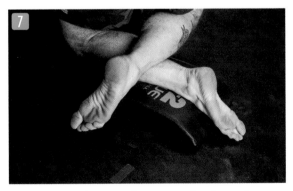

Drive your shin up the tissue, looking for knots to destroy.

Superfriend Shear

Working with a partner, you can focus on completely relaxing your body and letting your friend deal out the pain. Lie down with support underneath the front of your ankle, and have your friend work back and forth across the tissues of your lower leg.

Place an ab mat or a folded towel underneath your lower leg as you lie down in a prone position. Allow your Superfriend to set his foot into position.

Have your friend use his foot to work across the tissues near your ankle joint, starting with a smashing technique into the muscle and then working side to side across the grain of the muscle fiber.

Your buddy's foot can strip the muscle, working slowly up and down the length of the fibers.

Tack, Twist, & Floss

Place a ball on your heel cord and tack down the tissue, and then twist and floss the skin. You can use a lacrosse ball for this mobilization, but a softer ball with some grippiness to it will enable you to get a nice twist on the sliding surfaces. I'm using one of Jill Miller's Yoga Tune Up Therapy Balls.

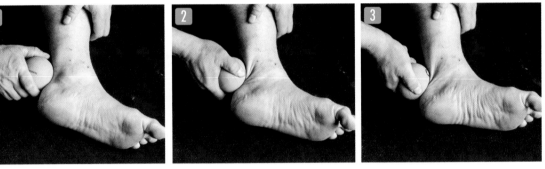

Place a Yoga Tune Up ball or other soft, grippy ball on the rear of your ankle.

Tack down some tissue layers and floss them by twisting the ball.

Moving up and down your heel cord, unglue the sliding surfaces by applying pressure, moving the ball back and forth across the cord, and twisting the tissues.

Lateral Ankle Smash & Floss

Place a ball between the outside of your heel/ankle and the floor. Use one hand to hold the ball in place and the other hand to move your foot through a full range of flexion to floss the sliding surfaces.

ALTERNATE ROTATION: Move your foot from side to side to get some lateral-medial action going.

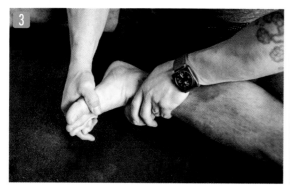

Place the ball on the lateral side of your ankle, applying pressure with your hand.

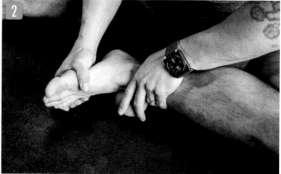

Use one hand to flex and extend your foot while continuing to press the ball into your ankle with the other hand.

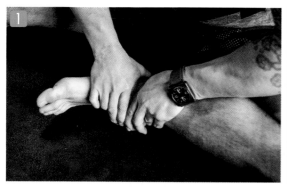

Notice how you can obtain greater depth by pressing your ankle into the ball and into the floor.

Rotate your foot from side to side as well as up and down. Hunt for spots that help you unglue the tissues and fascias and open up blood flow to the area.

Medial Ankle Smash & Twist

Your mission here is to breathe some life and sliding surface function into the fascias and tissues on the medial side (inside) of your ankle. Start with a spot underneath the talus bone.

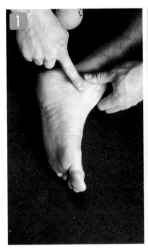

Pick a spot near the talus bone on the inside of your ankle.

Take a Yoga Tune Up Ball or other soft, grippy ball like a racquetball and tack the spot, then use twisting motions.

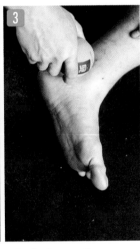

Work throughout the area in search of hotspots of matted-down tissue.

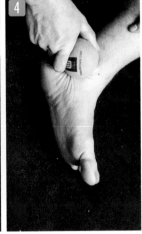

After you find a good nugget of tissue to work on, dig in deep and twist.

Two-Ball Smash & Floss

You'll be working your shins in this mobilization, but keep in mind that this work also does wonders for your feet, as the two are connected. Think of it like working on puppet strings. Place one ball between the bones of your lower leg (the lateral compartment) and the floor, and another ball on the inside of your shin (the anterior compartment). Dig into the tissue from above and below, moving up and down your shin. Say goodbye to shin splints!

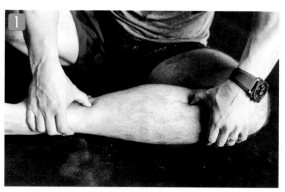

Prepare to work along your tibia.

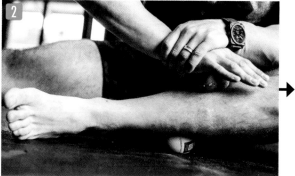

While pressing a ball into your tibia with your hands, place another ball between your fibula and the ground to get a double whammy.

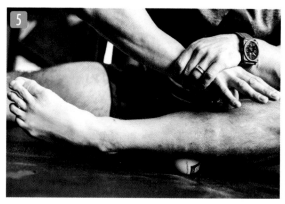

In addition to flexing and extending your foot, rotate your foot laterally.

Place both hands on the top ball to exert maximum force.

Roll the top ball from near your knee toward your ankle.

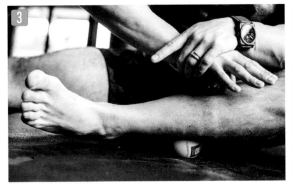

Lift your foot off the ground and contract-relax your ankle to get a deep flossing effect.

Work the top ball down your shin. As you move down your tibia, continue flexing and rotating your foot.

Double-Ball Ankle Smash & Strip

Although acute pains and aches from running can be expressed in the feet, an upstream problem is often the culprit. All of the tissues that control the movement of your feet are contained in your lower leg. So if you have arch pain, don't forget to create some slack by searching for trouble spots in your shins. This mobilization will dig in and let you know what's going on.

Use a double-lacrosse-ball setup or the Gemini. (In the photos I'm using a pair of Jill Miller's Yoga Tune Up Therapy Balls in their tote.)

Using your body weight to exert force, slowly strip the tissue, rolling your shin up and down between the balls.

FEET AND TOES

Plantar Mobilizations

Using a ball, spend a few minutes working up and down the arch and around your foot. Simply apply pressure wave motion (see page 191) using your body weight. Hunt down those messy little knots and spend some additional time working through that tissue. Are you watching *Game of Thrones*? It's a good time to get in some plantar work as well.

ALTERNATE TOOL: Use a roller to get some global shear.

The main rule of the game with plantar mobilizations is to actively search for acute hotspots in your foot and then use twisting forces, pressure waves, and smashes to invigorate the fascias, muscles, nerves, and other tissues that make up the leaf spring that is your foot.

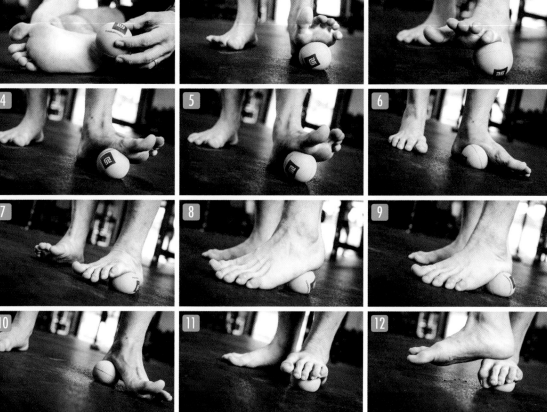

Dorsiflexion Work

Nothing says good morning to your toes like loaded dorsiflexion work. In a kneeling position, spend time rolling back on your toes and waking up the range of motion throughout.

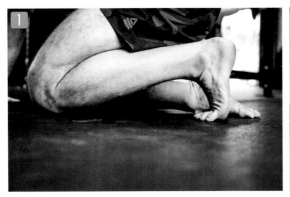

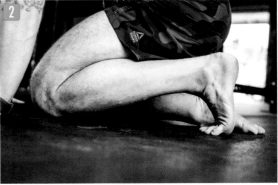

Kneel down like a sprinter getting into the blocks, and hold this position to start working the fascias and muscles of your foot.

Work from side to side, back and forth, and give each foot two minutes of love.

Plantar Flexion Overdrive

This one feels as gnarly as it looks. In a kneeling position, use contract-relax movements to invigorate the fascias in your feet and develop your plantar range of motion.

Seat yourself on the ground with one leg fully flexed and your foot in plantar flexion.

Lifting at the knee, you'll notice some rather remarkable fireworks going on in the fascias throughout the top of your foot.

Keep your foot and knee in alignment as you work toward maximum plantar flexion.

Hold your max position for two minutes on each side. After mobilizing one foot, check its range of motion against the range of motion of your other foot to note how much change you have achieved.

Toe Grip

The Toe Grip is similar to the plantar mobs, but this one really works on strengthening and spreading out your toes.

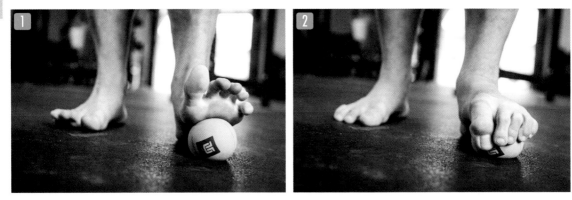

Open your toes wide.

Grab a ball with your toes like you would try to pick up a basketball with one hand.

Toe Re-animator

This mobilization is from Kit Laughlin, the creator of Stretch Therapy, and it's a badass way to wake up toes that have atrophied from years of wearing overbuilt shoes (see Chapter 5). Splice your fingers between your toes and work up and down, side to side, and in between. This is another good activity to complement TV watching.

Use the photos as a template for ideas. The primary idea here is to intertwine your fingers and toes.

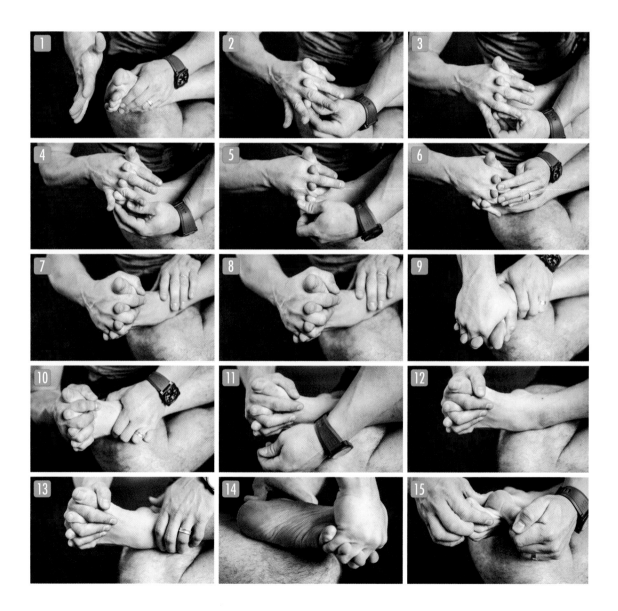

UPPER LEG

Adductor Smash

Your adductors are critical to achieving the stabilization you want to achieve each time one of your feet touches the ground. Runners tend to focus on the hamstrings, IT band, and quads and blow off the adductors. Your adductors help stabilize your back, so putting in some regular maintenance on them is going to help you. Use a pressure wave with a roller on the inside of your thigh.

Position your roller on the inside of your thigh and relax into it to get good depth. Drive the same-side hip toward the floor to deepen the pressure. Explore the adductor for tight spots to work your way into.

Anterior Hip Smash

This mobilization is an excellent tool to aid you in your pursuit of the standards related to optimal hip function (see Chapters 8 and 9). It's also a good way to alleviate lower back pain. Use a ball to smash your way into the deep tissues on the front and side of your thigh. Spend 10 minutes on one side, then stand up and compare it to the other side.

The starting place for working in these areas of the anterior and high glute is right at the top of your hip bone. If you've been putting in some mileage, the tissues in this area are probably a mess, and you'll know right away that you're going to feel this mobilization in a big way.

Press your body weight into the ball, and then roll back and forth through the mashed fibers.

Rotate your femur to get some twisting forces into the mobilization. And remember to *breathe*.

Hamstring Floss

Hamstrings are a runner's best friend, particularly if you're using the powerful muscles of your posterior chain (which is how you should run). Note that *hamstrings* is plural: You have three muscles that work together to flex your leg. They all deserve your attention. Using a box or chair and a roller, pressure wave your way through your hamstrings in search of knots and pockets of tight tissue. When you find those hotspots, give them special attention.

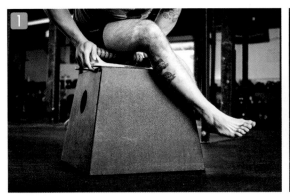

Using a box or other elevated surface on which you can get leverage, place the roller on your hamstrings.

Rotate, flex, and extend your leg to work the tissues from a variety of angles.

Hamstring Smash, Superfriend Version

This mobilization is not unlike a Thai massage—you relax into the ground while your training partner works up, down, and across your hamstrings.

 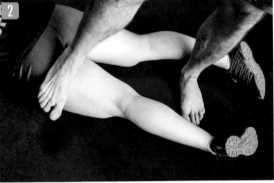

Have your buddy put his bare foot into your hamstring and work deep into and across your tissues.

Be sure that he works up into the high hamstring area.

Knee 360

Does your knee hurt? Using a double-lacrosse-ball setup for the outside and another ball for the inside, work around and above your knee to relieve the tissues that spend so much time stabilizing the joint.

Pictured on the left, a double-ball setup, and on the right, the Gemini. You can also tape together two lacrosse balls.

Position the tool so that you can begin working upstream of your knee.

Lean back and work through the tissues.

Rotate your leg and use a pressure wave.

Add a softball or Supernova to the inside of your upper leg to get some additional work around your knee.

Flex and extend your top leg to pressure wave through your adductor issues.

Knee Flexion Gap & Smash

This mobilization is an effective way to unglue the tissues behind your knee. It's also a great tool for dealing with tight calf muscles. Fold a ball into your knee joint and then flex your leg. Work through the tissues by moving your foot around and posting it underneath you to increase the pressure.

Seated on the floor, place a ball behind your knee.

Flex your leg around the ball to create a compression force into your tissues. Flex and extend your foot for additional work.

Patellar Smash & Floss

Lie down, place a ball above your knee, and begin exploring the tissues around your kneecap. Rotate your leg, flex and extend your lower leg and foot, and really unglue the area.

This mobilization (in concert with the other knee mobilizations) can do wonders to release tightness that is being expressed as pain. Prone on the floor, use a ball and your body weight to unmash the tissues around your kneecap.

Quad Smash, Superfriend Version

The benefit of having a friend dole out the mobility pain is that you can lie back, relax, and try to use mental distraction—think about your upcoming tropical vacation or something like that—while your tissues get a good lashing.

Have your friend put some weight through his foot into your quadriceps.

Work across the quad and up and down the front of your femur. Put extra time into those locations that trigger a pain face.

Work above your knee, across all your tissues. Relax into the roller and oscillate back and forth for an optimal effect.

Quad Smash Roller

With two minutes per side of a deep smash with a roller or Battlestar, you can take care of all the tight business that your training leaves behind in your quads.

TRUNK & HIPS

Banded Hip, Single-Leg Squat

This powerful hip opener is great for improving hip extension (see Chapter 9). The band creates a distraction that will help solve joint capsule restriction problems and enable you to move into a deeper position. Loop a band around the crease of your hip and walk backward to create as much tension as you reasonably can. Squeeze your butt and belly and lower your knee to the ground, as pictured. Repeat.

Facing a post, loop a band above your hip crease. Walk backward to get a lot of tension in the band. Squeeze your glutes as you set yourself up in the position that you would use to dip into a lunge.

With your glutes engaged, belly muscles tight, and torso upright, drop your knee toward the floor.

Return to the start by extending both legs.

Double-Band Hip Distraction

This mobilization is a powerful way to work on resetting the health and vitality of your hip capsule and a great part of your arsenal in working on your hip extension and flexion (see Chapters 8 and 9).

You'll need two bands for this one. Working on your right leg, loop one band around the front of your hip and the other around your foot. Now move your right leg both across your body and to the outside of your body.

Global Gut Smash

Even if you're using good positions when you run, it's likely that you're overworking your trunk due to the task of stabilizing your trunk. If you've ever been to a sports massage therapist who has dug into your psoas, you know in a visceral way how tight and painful it can be. So work your abs in a global fashion, but also get the psoas.

The psoas is a long muscle that originates in the lower lumbar spine and crosses through to the lower pelvis. It stabilizes the spine, flexes the hips, and helps generate power through rotation. Wham. In a runner, it takes a serious beating and gets really tight. Using a large, soft ball (like a half-inflated soccer ball), lie with the ball underneath your stomach, work through your abdominals, and also find that psoas (you'll feel it) and give it some time.

Use a deflated soccer ball or the like. I'm using the Coregeous Ball that Jill Miller designed expressly for this type of work.

Lie down on the ball, with the ball placed right in your gut. Take a big breath, hold it in for a bit, and then let it out, sinking into and around the ball as you relax. This will plumb the depth of your gut.

Work across your stomach, looking for those spots where you feel the heavens part. Contract and relax to inject some relief into your psoas.

Psoas Smash & Floss

For extra credit in working on your psoas, use a softball to really dig in.

Notice the location of the ball on my stomach—this is the pathway you'll plunge into to get to the psoas.

With your body weight channeled into the ball, work the left and right sides, searching for and discovering your psoas.

Glute Smash & Floss

A simple ball can penetrate deep into the hard-working muscles of the hip, including the deep rotator muscles. Optimal hip function is crucial for stability, injury prevention, and power output. The Glute Smash & Floss can pinpoint and help you attend to buried trigger points and hotspots. Using a softball or Supernova, place the ball on a box or chair and then sit on the ball. Apply as much weight as you can as you sift through your hip muscles.

Start at the lower hamstrings, just above your knee.

On a box, work all the way up to your hips, scouting for knotty tissues along the way.

When you find a hotspot, contract and relax those muscles, pressure wave back and forth, and sink into the tissues. Floss by flexing and extending your leg.

Glute Smash

For more targeted work, use a lacrosse ball on specific knots and floss through them.

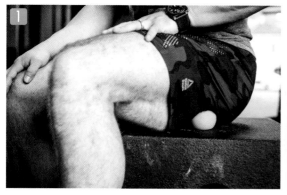 

Place a lacrosse ball or Yoga Tune Up Ball on your glutes.

When you find a particularly nasty area, rotate your leg back and forth across the ball.

Hip Capsule Rotation

Lots of running with poor form can create an impingement at the front of your hip and send you off the rails with limitations in your ability to walk and run with a neutral foot (see Chapter 4). This mobilization can help you reset your hip joint. Kneel on the ground with most of your weight on one knee. Your kneecap should be directly underneath your hip. Drop your hip to the outside and continue to load the weight on your knee. Move your torso forward and backward.

On your hands and knees, shift your weight onto one knee. Make sure that your hip and knee are aligned.

Pivot on your knee, driving your hip toward the ground, as if you were trying to use your femur to puncture a hole in your hip. This is where you're really getting into your hip capsule.

Move your trunk backward and then forward over your knee to work both ends of your hip capsule.

Posterior Chain Banded Floss

Using the banded floss technique, this is one of the best ways to maintain strong, healthy hamstrings and slide and glide within your tissues. The flossing action will help with hip position as well.

Facing away from a pole, loop a band around the front of your hip. Step forward to work up tension in the band. Place your hands on the ground in front of you and begin flexing and extending your leg.

Single Leg Flexion

This mobilization is a good one for developing and mastering your squatting ability, hip flexion, hip extension, and overall hip function. It doesn't require any equipment, which makes it a good choice to rotate into your schedule when you have a couple of minutes. As you get into the heart of the mobilization, really work your femur bone around and flatten your back to search for especially tight knots and corners surrounding your hip capsule, like you're using a can opener to open things up.

With one leg trailing behind you, post your forward foot on the ground.

Drop your rear knee and drive your hip toward the ground.

Drive with your hand as you extend your torso in the opposite direction.

Here's another look from above. Notice the can opener effect being applied to the hip.

Rotate your upper body inward, as pictured. Focus your attention on those spots in your hip that are especially tight.

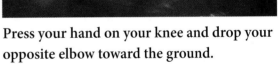

Press your hand on your knee and drop your opposite elbow toward the ground.

BACK

The target area is adjacent
to the lower lumbar. This is
where you want to start.

Low-Back Ball Smash

Running can wreak havoc on your lower back thanks to all
the pounding involved. Maintaining a neutral, engaged spine
is your first order of defense in preventing lower back pain.
But even then, you need to work in time to poke around
the tissues and triggers points of your lower back to keep it
healthy and powerful.

Place a ball along one side of your spine and lie down on
it. Extend the same-side arm above your head and use your
body weight to press into the tightened tissues surrounding
the lower lumbar.

This is a smash, so your first task is to lie
down on the ball and relax into it. Be sure to
breathe. Use the contract-relax technique to
allow even greater reach with the ball.

Begin to move around slowly on the ball,
creating a pressure wave on any gnarly bits
that you find.

Lift your hips off the ground to leverage more body weight onto the ball. Breathe and relax as you move the ball around your lower back, spending extra time on spots that are tight and knotted up.

Rotate your torso as you roll from side to side through your tissues on the ball.

T-Spine Global Smash

Lie with a roller or Battlestar positioned across your T-spine area, cross your arms in front of you, and globally work the area. Press into the floor with your legs to add to the bodyweight pressure. Rotate your torso from side to side.

If you recall from Chapter 6, many distance runners are messed up when it comes to the upper back and the flexibility of the thoracic spine. This results in that shoulders-rolling-forward problem that makes it impossible for athletes to use good posture when they run. It can also result in neck pain, because the head is usually thrust out in front of the body and has to be stabilized with muscles; the skeleton isn't able to do the work it is designed to do.

Freeing yourself of this problem starts with opening up your thoracic spine. This mobilization offers direct work to do so.

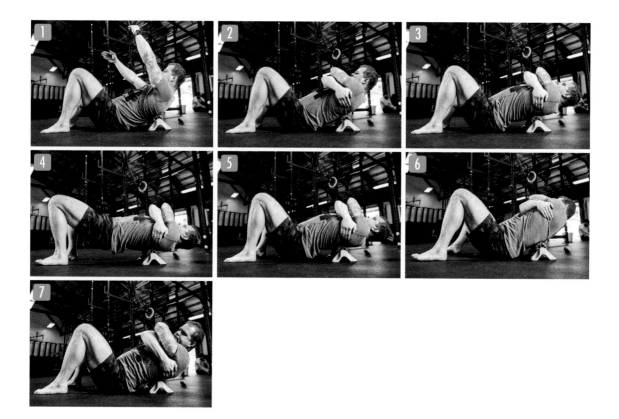

T-Spine Double-Ball Strip

For more specific work along your spine, use a double-lacrosse-ball setup or the Gemini to strip through the tissues connected to the vertebrae.

Place the tool (I'm using the Gemini) over your spine.

Lying down on the tool, roll so that it reaches the thoracic spine region. Hug your arms around your body to reduce the slack.

Pushing your feet into the ground and raising your hips, work the tool toward your upper back and the base of your neck.

Stop at each vertebra and work from side to side to unlock the tissue.

SHOULDERS

Anterior Shoulder

If the Supple Thoracic Spine standard is a goat for you, work on the front of your shoulders to help unshackle you from the poor posture and position that a stiff upper back can destroy you with.

This is your target area.

Lay into the front of your shoulder and extend your arm over your head.

Move your arm into a horizontal position and press your body weight into the ball.

Wrap your arm around your low back and press your body weight into the ball.

Banded Bully

As part of your work on your T-spine, work to reset your shoulder joints with this mobilization. Loop a band around the crease of your shoulder and lean your body weight into it. Turn your head to the side to deepen the mob.

Loop the band around your shoulder and drive away from the post to create tension in the band and distraction in the joint. Feel your shoulder being pulled back into the joint capsule.

Wrap your arm around your lower back and grab it with your opposite hand.

Raise your arm out away from your back.

Turn your head to the side to get additional flossing of the tissues in the region.

28-DAY SAMPLE MOBILITY OVERHAUL PLAN

Every athlete is different, and every athlete has his or her own set of strengths and weaknesses to deal with. My primary mission as a teacher is—as the saying goes—to teach you how to fish rather than grill up a plate of salmon for you. My goal is to encourage and empower you with a system of maintenance that puts you in charge.

That said, here is a sample 28-day plan of how you might install the *Ready to Run* approach into your life. The idea is to spend at least 10 minutes a day, every day, on solving your mobility problems. In the course of four weeks, you should visit each area of your body—feet and lower legs, upper legs, hips and trunk, and upper back—at least once. When it comes to weaknesses you've identified, I want you to drop in even more frequently.

During this 28-day period, you should also be managing your lifestyle issues. Are you hydrating enough every day? Are you making neutral feet a permanent habit? Are you managing any hotspots that flare up? These might seem like little extras, but they're not. It's these lifestyle errors (I also call them adaptive errors) that are the source of the river of injuries that drive runners and other athletes crazy.

Remember that if you're stressed for time, you should search out ways to build mobilizations into your day. Make them a part of your warm-up or cool-down, and bulldoze through any reluctance to do mobility work in public—when you're waiting to board a flight, for example. Don't be shy. Be mobile and Ready to Run.

	MONDAY	TUESDAY	WEDNESDAY
WEEK 1	Couch Stretch (page 114), 2 minutes per side. Booster: Work on shins with Two-Ball Smash & Floss (page 214), 2 minutes on each leg.	Voodoo Tuesday (see below). Booster: Squat Test #1 (page 92) and #2 (page 96), followed by 2 minutes of Low-Back Ball Smash (page 242).	Plantar Blitzkrieg (see below). Booster: Test the Hip Flexion standard (page 105), then take a ball to any stiff tissues impinging your hip range of motion.
WEEK 2	Couch Stretch (page 114), 2 minutes per side. Booster: Hip Flexion Test (page 105).	Voodoo Tuesday (see below). Booster: Double-Ball Ankle Smash & Strip (page 216), 2 minutes on each leg.	Psoas Smash & Floss (page 234), 2–4 minutes. Booster: Plantar Blitzkrieg (see below).
WEEK 3	Couch Stretch (page 114). Booster: Calf Smash & Pressure Wave (page 205), 2 minutes on each leg.	Voodoo Tuesday (see below). Booster: T-Spine Global Smash (page 244) and Anterior Shoulder (page 246).	Plantar Blitzkrieg (see below). Booster: Dorsiflexion Work (page 218).
WEEK 4	Couch Stretch (page 114), 2 minutes per side. Booster: Hamstring Floss (page 224), 2 minutes on each leg.	Voodoo Tuesday (see below). Booster: Global Gut Smash (page 233).	Jumping and Landing Test #1 (page 172) and #2 (page 174). Booster: Banded Bully (page 247).

Voodoo Tuesday. Get out your VooDoo Floss Band and wrap any hotspot (tired or tender area), be it your foot, ankle, knee, calf, or hamstring. Spent at least 2 minutes wrapped up and moving the limb through its full range of motion.

Plantar Blitzkrieg. Spend at least 10 minutes dousing your feet with plantar mobilizations: Toe Grip (page 220) and Toe Re-animator (page 221). Really bring them back to life.

Bracing Sequence Drill. On the hour during your waking hours, stop what you're doing, check to make sure that your feet are in a neutral position, and then go through the bracing sequence (page 65).

THURSDAY	FRIDAY	SATURDAY	SUNDAY
Bracing Sequence Drill (see below). Booster: Adductor Smash (page 222), 2 minutes on each leg.	Goat Herding (see below). Booster: 1 hour or more in compression socks.	Barefoot Saturday (see below). Booster: Toe Re-animator (page 221).	T-Spine Global Smash (page 244) and Double-Ball Strip (page 245). Booster: Lifestyle Supplies Check (see below).
Hamstring Floss (page 224), 2 minutes on each leg. Booster: Couch Stretch (page 114), 2 minutes per side.	Goat Herding (see below). Booster: 1 hour or more in compression socks.	Barefoot Saturday (see below). Booster: Ankle Range of Motion Test #1 (page 124) and #2 (page 126), followed by Medial Ankle Smash & Twist (page 213).	Warm-up/Cool-down Workshop: Tinker with your warm-up and cool-down. Add jumping rope to your warm-up and the mobilization of your choice to your cool-down.
Jumping and Landing Test #1 (page 172) and #2 (page 174). Booster: Bone Saw Calf Smash (page 208).	Goat Herding (see below). Booster: Knee Flexion Gap & Smash (page 227).	Barefoot Saturday (see below). Booster: Plantar Flexion Overdrive (page 219).	T-Spine Global Smash (page 244) and Anterior Shoulder (page 246). Booster: Lifestyle Supplies Check (see below).
Plantar Blitzkrieg (see below). Booster: Glute Smash (page 236), 2 minutes per side.	Goat Herding (see below). Booster: Anterior Hip Smash (page 223). Double Booster: Watching a movie at home tonight? Have a glass of wine and spend 2 minutes holding the Couch Stretch on each side.	Barefoot Saturday (see below). Booster: Toe Re-animator (page 221). Bonus: Work at a desk and sit a lot? Seriously consider changing your life for the better by buying or building a standing desk.	Squat practice: Get into a good squat position and gather a total of 10 minutes in that position. Booster: 1 hour in compression socks.

Goat Herding. Refer to your testing and pick out one or more standards that are your goats, or weaknesses. Perhaps you have upper back mobility issues (Standard #3, A Supple Thoracic Spine) or wretched heel cords (Standard #7, Ankle Range of Motion), or your squatting technique (Standard #4) needs work. Dedicate Goat Herding time to working on those weaknesses, knowing that as you evolve them into strengths, you'll gain in injury prevention and performance.

Barefoot Saturday. Spend as much of the day as you can being barefoot.

Lifestyle Supplies Check. Take some time to inventory your mobility tools and assess your need for flat shoes, compression socks, or electrolytes. Make sure that you have the stuff you need for the coming week. Also plot out your weekly goal in regard to transitioning to flat shoes (if you haven't done so already). See page 76 for a plan to transition smartly and safely.

PART 4

You have the mindset, you have the tools, and you have the talent. Where to now? In these final pages, I want to give you some weaponry. Engaging the 12 standards with focus, lifestyle changes, and mobility work is your starting point, but the life of an athlete is never without new challenges to confront, work through, and learn from. Let's talk a bit about some particular and common injury problems that running tends to serve up, and about how to get the most value out of the sports medicine world that's out there waiting to help as you continue to push the envelope.

CHAPTER 18
ATTACKING COMMON RUNNING INJURIES

By now you should understand that running injuries aren't some mystery of another universe. They are physics and biology in action. See them as messages about what's missing in your mechanics, your range of motion, and your potential to run faster, longer, and better.

This chapter will be somewhat of a review of the information presented earlier in this book, but I want to give you the basic attack plan for several common running injuries so that you can see how the *Ready to Run* mobility template can be wielded against any chronic pain that arises from running. It's a two-stage plan, but you can enact both stages simultaneously:

1. When chronic pain rears its ugly head, study your mechanics and positions to determine the root cause(s) of the problem. Realize that a pain in the arch of your foot can be an expression of weakness and imbalance in your glutes and lower back, for example. Go through the position standards: neutral feet, a good squat, hip flexion, hip extension, and the mobility of your feet and ankles.

2. Position and mechanics come first; treating the symptoms is your second priority. Work on the problem area, but also above and below the problem,

or "upstream and downstream." If you have a knee pain, for example, spend time each day working below (calves) and above (hamstrings, quads, glutes). The idea is to give the problem area some breathing room by creating slack. Feed slack into the system, use VooDoo Floss Band compression (see page 150) for any hotspot inflammation, and work on those sticky sliding surfaces on the hotspot.

If, after you've done this work, you're not seeing a change (although you likely will), it's time to take an account of what you've tried and the results and have a talk with your trusted sports medicine healthcare provider.

To give you a snapshot of how to use this approach, here are some common chronic running injuries and how you might work on each of them.

PLANTAR FASCIITIS

Plantar fasciitis, the debilitating scourge of runners and athletes everywhere. The plantar fascia is a big sheet of connective tissue on the bottom of the foot. It is shaped like a triangle and tapers into the heel, where it connects to the heel bone.

Plantar fasciitis is sort of a catchall phrase for any chronic pain in this area of the foot. It could be from a nerve ending getting caught, for example, or an inflamed bursa sac. The bottom line is that it hurts every time you plant your foot on the ground, which does real wonders for your running.

When you have pain, you need to attack the problem like the athlete you are. Your first order of business is to begin analyzing the underlying cause within your mechanics. Heel strikers everywhere are courting chronic arch pain on a daily basis. It can also be a manifestation of weak hips and poor midline stability.

Also pay attention to the dorsiflexion and plantar flexion of your foot—if you're short in your range of motion (as testing for Standard #7 will reveal), then this is going to feed into arch pain. If plantar fasciitis is on your resume, then make the Ankle Range of Motion standard a priority.

To alleviate the immediate issue, you need to work upstream and downstream of the problem. This means selecting mobility exercises that treat your toes, particularly the mobility of your big toe, as well as your heel cords and calf muscles. Doing so will start giving slack to the system.

Also, get your Voodoo Floss Band involved to speed the healing process. Perform VooDoo Floss Band compression (see page 150). Wrap up your arch and spend a few minutes flexing and pointing your foot. This will floss through the sliding surfaces and aid your lymphatic system.

It's also time to use a Yoga Tune Up ball or lacrosse ball directly on the tissues of your arch. Refer to the foot exercises beginning on page 217.

Look for those ropy hotspots that are shortening your system. Roll deeply into these places. You need to get some suppleness back into the arch of your foot. Build this work into your day, but first and foremost do it before getting out of bed and putting weight on your bare foot. Think of it as adhering to the Warming Up standard.

ILIOTIBIAL BAND SYNDROME

Like plantar fasciitis, IT band syndrome is another catchall name for injuries related to the IT band. It usually refers to a hotspot of pain on the outside of the knee. It's also usually a runner's problem.

The IT band is crazy. I recall my amazement at how thick it was when I peeled one out of a cadaver for the first time. It attaches to basically everything—your glutes, your hamstrings, and your quads.

So study your mechanics. Look for movement faults. IT band syndrome is usually a result of weak hips and a valgus knee problem where the joint is collapsing inward and you're swinging your foot around for a wretched heel strike.

Don't think that you can "stretch out" the IT band. It's so heavy-duty that you could use it to suspend a Volkswagen! Instead, feed slack back into the system by working upstream and downstream of the problem. Really dig into your high hip area, the side of your hip in particular. You can also generate slack by mobilizing your hamstring and quads (see pages 224, 225, and 229). Use VooDoo Floss Band compression (see page 150) on any inflamed hotspots.

Place a ball in the crook of your knee and flex your leg around it for some flexion gapping (see page 192) for relief. Beware of the neuromuscular bundle behind your knee—if you feel a weird, nervy pain, back off and move the ball. You don't want to mess with that.

RUNNER'S KNEE

This rotten ailment causes pain on the inside of the knee with each footfall. Let's start with mechanics. Runner's knee is often an expression of—you guessed it—poor mechanics. The foot isn't neutral, the knee collapses inward, and you mess with the connective tissues and cartilage within the joint.

Fix your position and support it by looking for missing range of motion—namely hip flexion and hip extension.

Perform VooDoo Floss Band compression (see page 150) around your knee, moving the joint through its full range of motion. Mobilize upstream and downstream to open up slack—calves, shins, hamstrings, quads—and blast into those glutes.

SHIN SPLINTS

Shin splints are a nasty affliction for runners, soccer players, basketball players, and other athletes who engage in sports that involve a lot of running, especially on a hard surface like a track or court.

You should know the plan by now: Examine your positions and mechanics and work on fixing them. Get out that VooDoo Floss Band, wrap it around the problem area, and spend some time pointing and flexing your foot.

Speaking of dorsiflexion and plantar flexion—pepper your mobility work with lower leg and hip mobilizations.

Place a lacrosse ball between your shin and the ground (check the mobility exercises on this—see pages 214–216) and slowly work that anterior compartment, up and down between your ankle and your knee.

Finally, create slack upstream and downstream by working on your heel cord, the bottom of your foot, your big toe, and your upper leg.

CHAPTER 19
TURBOCHARGED SPORTS MEDICINE

I want to assure you of two principles that I completely believe in and hope you take away from this book. At first glance, these principles seem to be at right angles to one another, but in fact they work together like the alloy of iron and carbon.

Principle #1: All human beings should be able to perform basic maintenance on themselves.

Your first step on the journey toward higher performance and injury prevention is to understand and appreciate how much value you can get out of just 10 to 15 minutes a day of working toward achieving and maintaining the standards presented in this book. It's not the job of a sports medicine professional or a running shoe salesperson to take care of your tissues and joints, the positions you practice throughout the day, whether you hydrate or not, and whether you're actively working toward retaining normal ranges of motion in your feet, ankles, legs, hips, and back. It's your job, and you want it to be your job. By accepting this responsibility, you'll immediately gain several things:

- You can be on this job 24 hours a day.
- You will get an invaluable education from exploring your mechanics, unveiling problems, and creating mobilizations of your own.

- You will learn a new, individualized language of movement and mechanics that will come into play during training and in the toughest moments of a challenging endurance event. When your form starts to fall to pieces, you'll know how to reorganize in a way that will keep you going.

Finally, this knowledge will equip you well when you do need to visit a physical therapist, clinic, or sports massage therapist. Rather than just filling out an insurance form and off-loading the problem to someone else, you'll be able to ensure that you're getting what you're paying for.

Which leads us to the second principle:

Principle #2: When you visit a chiropractor, physical therapist, sports medicine clinic, or other body worker, go in with some hard-won knowledge to share.

When the PT asks what you have done so far to deal with the problem, be ready to answer with a list—the mobilizations you've been working on, the use of compression, changes in your mechanics, and anything else you've tried in performing basic maintenance on yourself.

First of all, this list will blow the therapist's mind. Why? Because I can tell you from experience. I always ask my physical therapy clients this question, and almost every time they answer with one sad and empty word: "Nothing."

If you go into a clinic with a couple of pages from your training journal in hand that detail what you've tried, what's worked, and what hasn't worked, then your PT is going to have a 100-mile head start in helping you solve the problem. It's going to empower her with so much quality information that she will be able to zero in.

So, yes, I want you to take the challenge of performing basic maintenance on your body, but this doesn't mean that I want you to avoid clinicians. Rather, the ideal scenario is to find a physiotherapist who is very good and very committed to helping you achieve optimal health and performance, and then develop a long-term relationship and a running dialogue.

Another reason for the No Days Off policy (see page 187) is that your battle to realize all 12 standards presented in this book and achieve optimal mobility is never over. It's a lifelong process. And enlisting the help of a trusted expert who has a stake in your long-term health and performance is invaluable. Not only will you get a lot more bang for your healthcare buck, but the process should also help you steer clear of some of the major problems that can convert a runner into a specialist on the elliptical trainer.

So take up this challenge: The next time you plan a visit to a sports medicine professional, go in with as much information as you can about the maintenance work you are doing. Go in with the challenge of blowing her mind. When she sees how committed you are to doing the work, you'll get that much more thought and effort in return.

A PARTING WORD

Not long ago, a sound engineer based in San Francisco trained for and ran in the Avenue of the Giants half-marathon through the redwood forests of northern California. A husband and father of two daughters, he saw the training and the event as part of a concentrated return to the health and fitness that he had lost while attending to the demands of young children and a job that, when deadlines came around, had him working long hours hunched over the sound board. He loved the training. He loved the community he found at the race. He couldn't find the right pacer in the race and ended up going on feel—which turned out to be faster than he intended. He hit the wall during the last miles, but he had built up such a buffer in the first half of the race that it didn't matter. He beat his goal, finishing in under two hours.

It was an all-around win—except for one thing: He contracted a case of shin splits. The engineer was unable to resume his running because of the splicing pain that shot up through his lower leg with each foot strike.

So, in an experience that is common to a lot of runners, CrossFitters, and athletes of all stripes, he went to see his doctor. He described his problem and the pain.

The doctor's response? (Can you guess?) A shrug of the shoulders and the following prescription:

"Stop running."

Relatively new to running, the sound engineer thought: *Geez. Is that it? Am I already done?*

No, he's not.

To add a little further thought to the preceding chapter, as an athlete, you need to make a distinction when it comes to seeing an MD for a problem or pain. If you have a weird, sketchy pain or illness, a visit to your physician is how you take severe illness possibilities off the table. Is an ache in your foot related to some mild inflammation in your heel or a stress fracture? Or, if you have deep pain in your femur, you want to make sure that you're not dealing with bone cancer.

But once you've taken such health-threatening (or life-threatening) possibilities off the table and you know that it's a nagging pain due to the running-related beating you've given yourself, you can ignore the doctor's advice to stop running. As super-running MD Tim Noakes advises, never take such advice as final if it's coming from a doctor who is not an athlete.

In the case of the sound engineer, it would be ridiculous for him to dump his newfound love of being an athlete because of a bout of shin splints. A simple and effective fix for him is going to start with developing neutral feet and adding some strength and suppleness to the tissues of his feet and ankles (jumping rope and spending some time smashing and flossing those tissues would be helpful first steps). But unfortunately, he'll have to sort through a lot of confusing information before deciding what to do. Some people might tell him that he should stop running. Others will tell him, "You need different running shoes."

To come full circle, I want to emphasize again that you, as an athlete, have the power to attend to 90 percent of your maintenance needs on your own. Sure, you want to deal with the symptoms, but you have to invest time and effort in effecting the deep repairs to your mechanics, the positions you use, and your ability to get into those positions.

As an athlete, you need to make a distinction when it comes to seeing an MD for a problem or pain. Once you've taken health-threatening (or life-threatening) possibilities off the table, then you can ignore the doctor's advice to stop running.

I've thrown a lot of information at you and made a lot of requests of you in this book. Both the general concepts and the demands embedded in the 12 standards I've tasked you to chase may seem overwhelming. And I know that asking you to wedge even 10 minutes into your day, every day, might set off an alarm. Here you are again, being asked to do one more thing. But I'm confident that if you play around with some of these ideas and techniques, you'll find the rewards energizing. You'll want to do more and learn more and experiment more.

I don't want you to close this book without at least getting this taste and the traction therein. So if time is one thing you have very, very little of, please at least commit to one week of this work. Take it for a test run. I'm asking for only a few minutes each day. I want you to give the work your best effort and pay attention to the changes you feel. I'm confident that once you gain some exposure to it, you'll want to make the time to dedicate yourself to the program full blast.

You can go through this week to get a feel for what the movement and mobility program is all about, and then, if you sense some positive changes and want to go deeper, you can spring right into testing yourself against the standards and beginning the journey toward being Ready to Run.

SAMPLE WEEK OF MOVEMENT AND MOBILITY WORK

MONDAY	TUESDAY	WEDNESDAY	THURSDAY
Hip extension: Couch Stretch (page 114), 2 minutes on each side.	Hip function: Spend a total of 4 minutes in a squat position, using a pole for support if necessary.	Feet: Plantar Mobilizations (page 217), 2 minutes on each foot.	Lateral Ankle Smash & Floss (page 212) and Medial Ankle Smash & Twist (page 213).
Drink 100 oz. of water, at least some of it spiked with electrolytes.	Drink 100 oz. of water, at least some of it spiked with electrolytes.	Drink 100 oz. of water, at least some of it spiked with electrolytes.	Drink 100 oz. of water, at least some of it spiked with electrolytes.
Work on the bracing sequence (page 65). Do it at least 3 times.	Make sure that you warm up before your workout and cool down afterward.	Wear flat shoes for at least a few hours during work or at home.	During the day, while at work or at home, throw in a Couch Stretch (page 114) while you're on the phone or watching TV. Build this bit of work—2 minutes on each side—into your daily routine.

FRIDAY	SATURDAY	SUNDAY
T-Spine Global Smash (page 244) and Hamstring Floss (page 224).	Barefoot Saturday (page 71) and Quad Smash Roller (page 230).	Glute Smash & Floss (page 235).
Drink 100 oz. of water, at least some of it spiked with electrolytes.	Drink 100 oz. of water, at least some of it spiked with electrolytes.	Drink 100 oz. of water, at least some of it spiked with electrolytes.
Add the mobility exercise of your choice to your post-workout cool-down.	Work on the bracing sequence again. Your goal is 5 times today.	Grab a beer and hang out with friends or family and enjoy some hot tub time. If you don't have access to a hot tub, try a nice, hot bath.

RUNNING POWER:
YOUR CONTINUING EDUCATION

Running is the movement that links athletes together. You play football, you run. You're a triathlete, you run. You're a CrossFitter, you run. You throw the Frisbee, you run. But a common problem is that an athlete puts in the time to refine all the various other skills involved in his or her sport but doesn't give running the same brand of study. There seems to be a belief that, *Hey, I'm fit from all the training; my running is good enough.* But you and I both know that if you are not meeting the 12 standards—if you don't have enough ankle range of motion or you're lacking hip function—you can't run well. And if you can't run well, you can't run fast, or you can't run at all because you're injured.

Your pursuit and maintenance of the *Ready to Run* standards will be an ongoing process, and it will require you to be creative, thoughtful, and attentive. Do you need to max out all 12 standards to realize your running talent? Maybe not, but there's something to be said for grabbing as much as you can. When I get in the car for a drive, I prefer to have a full tank of gas, even if I'm just going across town. There's a buffer involved, and it frees me up to think and work on other things.

So let's talk about your continuing education. Where do you go from here? After you're on the road to meeting the 12 standards, invest in a CrossFit Endurance or Pose Tech seminar and commit to mastering your mechanics. Being

Ready to Run, you'll be able to use the right positions to master the correct patterns of movement. It's a killer one-two punch.

Second, keep checking in at MobilityWOD.com. It's the place where we take the conversations we have at the dinner table—conversations about solving athletic performance problems and realizing human potential—and play around with the ideas we come up with. The following are some of the classic MWODs that will help you dial in the underlying concepts and techniques of this book.

Unglue Your Sticks

A full-scale attack on the sliding surface dysfunction and all-around stiffness that tend to plague athletes who put in a lot of running, jumping, and landing work. This is how you unglue it all.

www.mobilitywod.com/2010/11/episode-85-unglue-your-sticks-man/

Extension Dimension

Being tight in the high hip area can lead to limitations in how well you can internally rotate that leg. If extension and internal rotation are suffocating, you'll have a difficult time using your hamstring properly, and your foot will tend to swing and sway in abnormal, power-leaking patterns. This video shows you how to loosen it up.

www.mobilitywod.com/2011/01/episode-151365-runnersplit-jerk-dream.html

Smoking Brakes

Running downhill tends to burn out your quads and the accompanying muscles that take a beating from hard, hilly runs. Here's the antidote.

www.mobilitywod.com/2010/09/episdoe-23-runners-legs/

Dehydration Nation

As I've said, you are a system of systems. Where there's smoke, there's fire, and where there's fire, there are dehydrated, beef jerky–like calf muscles. It's time to kill the thirst.

www.mobilitywod.com/2011/04/episode-213365-recovering-your-jumping-calves.html

Your Springs

If you want to understand why your feet can get so mashed up, consider all the work they do. Then take an anatomy class and skin a cadaver's foot to understand how much is going on in there. Or watch this video.

www.mobilitywod.com/2011/04/episode-220365-lower-leg-business.html

Heel Cord Love

Going to a CrossFit Endurance or Pose Method seminar? Get ready by watching this video and preparing your lower legs for the sea change to come.

www.mobilitywod.com/2011/04/episode-237365-heel-cord-love.html

Medial Chain Business

I talk a lot about the posterior chain, but let's not forget about the medial chain—the groin and inner thigh—and what goes on terms of overall mechanics: systems of systems of systems.

www.mobilitywod.com/2011/05/episode-241365-sumo-and-medial-chain-business.html

Hamstring Heaven

Stretching is tired. Need to breathe some power into your hamstrings? Grab a Superfriend and prepare for your new legs.

www.mobilitywod.com/2011/06/episode-272365-tj-murphy-edition-and-hamstring-stiffness.html

IT Band and the Kitchen Sink

If you have a so-called "IT band problem," watch this video before you freak out about the shoes you're wearing.

www.mobilitywod.com/2010/10/episode-61-it-band-hell-and-help/

Squat Power

If you think that attaining the squatting standard is beyond you, tell it to my aunt—a five-time Ironman Masters triathlete who understands how to do the squat test with the ultimate Paleo timer (since Cavemen didn't have clocks).

www.mobilitywod.com/2011/02/episode-181-10-minute-squat-test-6/

Brian MacKenzie Warm-up

CrossFit Endurance super-coach and ultrarunner Brian MacKenzie can get your warm-up squared away.

www.mobilitywod.com/2012/03/warm-up-brian-mackenzie-running-warm-up/

RESOURCES

BOOKS

Becoming a Supple Leopard: The Ultimate Guide to Resolving Pain, Preventing Injury, and Optimizing Athletic Performance by Kelly Starrett with Glen Cordoza (Victory Belt, 2013). My first book, this *New York Times* bestseller explores the entire universe of the movement and mobility system for athletes of all types, shapes, and sizes. It investigates the underlying concepts used in *Ready to Run* in detail.

Power, Speed, Endurance: A Skill-Based Approach to Endurance Training by Brian MacKenzie with Glen Cordoza (Victory Belt, 2012). Brian MacKenzie's comprehensive training philosophy in regard to movement, running, cycling, and swimming.

Free+Style: Maximize Sport and Life Performance with Four Basic Movements by Carl Paoli with Anthony Sherbondy (Victory Belt, 2014). Another *New York Times* bestseller offering a road map for developing your ability to create movement with superstar coach Carl Paoli.

Born to Run: A Hidden Tribe, Superathletes, and the Greatest Race the World Has Never Seen by Christopher McDougall (Random House, 2011). You've probably read it, considering how long it's been selling like mad, but if you haven't, you're in for a treat. The primary narrative investigates the Tarahumara Indians (the otherworldly ultrarunnining superathletes mentioned in the title), spawning a series of investigations into the truth about running shoes, nutrition, the value of all-around athleticism for runners, and the unfolding universe of why running mechanics matter.

The Power of Habit: Why We Do What We Do in Life and Business by Charles Duhigg (Random House, 2011). Duhigg looks at the neurodynamics of habitual routines, triggers, and responses. How, Duhigg asks, are habits formed, unformed, and reformed? Ultimately the *New York Times* reporter provides an understanding of how we can effectively pry ourselves away from destructive choices by replacing them with better, healthier patterns. Want to make a better decision? This is how you do it for good.

The Sports Gene: Inside the Science of Extraordinary Athletic Performance by David Epstein (Current Trade, 2014). A fascinating exploration of how athletes navigate their way toward optimal expression of their athletic talent.

The Story of the Human Body by Daniel Lieberman (Vintage, 2014). The famed evolutionary biologist lays out the overpowering scientific truths showing how human beings—although slow compared to many mammals—have been engineered into the best distance runners on Earth.

Unbreakable Runner by Brian MacKenzie and T.J. Murphy (Velo Press, 2014). Training plans, from 5k to ultramarathon, using CrossFit Endurance founder Brian MacKenzie's low-mileage combination of skill, strength, and stamina.

WEBSITES

CrossFitEndurance.com. Find answers to your questions about orchestrating your mechanics work, strength training, and running into a composite approach. It's a massive and valuable resource afor those making the transition into a skill-based program.

MobilityWOD.com. Offering hundreds of archived videos, with new ones being created almost daily, the MWOD has become an engine behind new ideas and answers to performance-related problems in the sports world.

PoseMethod.com. The website of Dr. Nicholas Romanov, the one true pioneer of describing and teaching running mechanics and the creator of the Pose Method of running.

RogueFitness.com. An online superstore for upgrading the home mobility gym.

YogaTuneUp.com. Fascia expert Jill Miller's website is a great source of information, tools, and media products.

ABOUT THE AUTHORS

Dr. Kelly Starrett, coach and physiotherapist, is the author of the *New York Times* and *Wall Street Journal* bestseller *Becoming a Supple Leopard,* which has revolutionized how coaches, athletes, and everyday humans approach performance as it relates to movement, mechanics, and the actualization of human and athletic potential. He and his wife, Juliet Starrett, co-founded San Francisco CrossFit and MobilityWOD.com, where they share their innovative approach to movement, mechanics, and mobility with millions of athletes and coaches around the world. Kelly travels the world teaching his wildly popular CrossFit Movement & Mobility Course and also works with elite military forces and every branch of the military; athletes from the NFL, NBA, NHL, and MLB; and nationally ranked and world-ranked strength and power athletes. He consults with Olympic teams and universities and is a featured speaker at strength and conditioning and medical conferences nationwide. Kelly believes that all human beings should know how to move and be able to perform basic maintenance on themselves. He lives in northern California with his insanely talented and amazing wife and their two young lionesses, Georgia and Caroline. His chief life goal is to spend more time on the beach with his family.

T.J. Murphy, over the course of a 20-year career, has established himself as one of the endurance world's most prolific writers. Among his many roles as a magazine editor, he has served as editor-in-chief of both *Triathlete* and *Inside Triathlon* magazines and as editorial director of *Competitor* magazine. His endurance journalism has appeared in *Outside* and *Runner's World.* In 2012 he gave things a twist when he chronicled his personal odyssey into strength, conditioning, and mobility in the seminal work *Inside the Box: How CrossFit® Shredded the Rules, Stripped Down the Gym, and Rebuilt My Body.* He lives in Boston with the love of his life and inspiration, Gretchen Weber, and their baby boy, Milo Murphy, who never misses a chance to show off his sensational powers of mobility. (www.tjmurphy.net)

ACKNOWLEDGMENTS

First among the people responsible for the completion of this project whom I need to thank is T.J. Murphy. Still my most famous friend, now I will have to add "most talented and able friend" to that moniker. If the world really understood your rain-man-like abilities to both write and regurgitate esoteric running lore, you would be persecuted as the real-life Professor Charles Xavier genius-mutant you really are. Thank you for your kindness, flexibility, friendship, talent, and incredible ability to turn the boat around and head directly into the storm. And Gretchen Weber, don't think we aren't aware that you are the keel that keeps that boat from blowing off course and onto the rocks.

Thanks also to Brian MacKenzie, who gave me back running and introduced me to T.J. I appreciate that you knew how special I was that I could simultaneously pull and heel strike while wearing 40-pound shoes. Your faith and ability to teach such a foundational human skill, when so many people couldn't see the forest for the trees, has literally given countless people back a chunk of their humanity. Who knew that your life's work was really about standing in the breach on behalf of those of us who didn't know any better? If this is really a book about public health, then you are the guy who showed me I didn't have to run in squalor.

Tom Wiscombe, you may be the only true genius I know. I am so grateful that the older brother I always longed for is actually related to me, and freaky talented. Juliet and I would be greatly diminished without your voice, eye, honesty, and advocacy.

Dave Beatie, Susan Crane, and Christopher Jerard are the spine and vital organs of MWOD. An organism is pretty worthless if it can't interact with its environment and take care of itself. We wouldn't be able to perform either function without you. I'm not sure how we tricked you all onto the team, but I'm glad we did.

Darren Miller and John Segesta, thank you for leveraging your considerable talents to make this book so damn sexy.

Thank you to the many professionals that we interviewed, quoted, or stood on the shoulders of to make this book more than it otherwise could have been.

And finally, thank you to my family for the love and support required to be modern, working-adult humans *and* raise two amazing girls.

INDEX